THREE
BLOKES
IN A
DODGE

Mark Brennand

THREE BLOKES IN A DODGE

A clockwise journey around the American South West

by

Mark Brennand

NEWBRIDGE PRESS

Bibliography

Bill Bryson: *The Lost Continent. Travels in Small Town America* (Abacus 1990)

J D Dickey, Nick Edwards, Paul Whitfield and Mark Ellwood: *The Rough Guide to California* (Rough Guides 2008)

The publisher and author have done their best to ensure the accuracy and currency of all the information in *Three Blokes in a Dodge*. However they can accept no responsibility for any loss, injury or inconvenience sustained by any traveller as a result of information or advice contained in the book.

First published in 2009 by Newbridge Press,
Coign Chambers, 1 Newbridge Avenue, WV6 0LW

ISBN 13: 978-0-9563499-0-3

Printed in the UK by Short Run Press, Exeter

To Catherine

Lincolnshire County Council	
04621485	
Askews	
ADV	£4.89
	0918534/0001

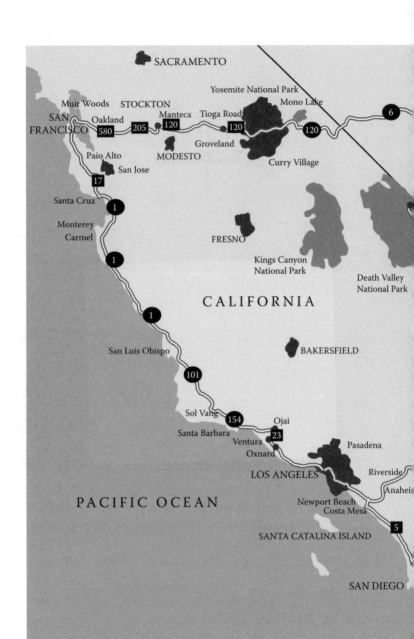

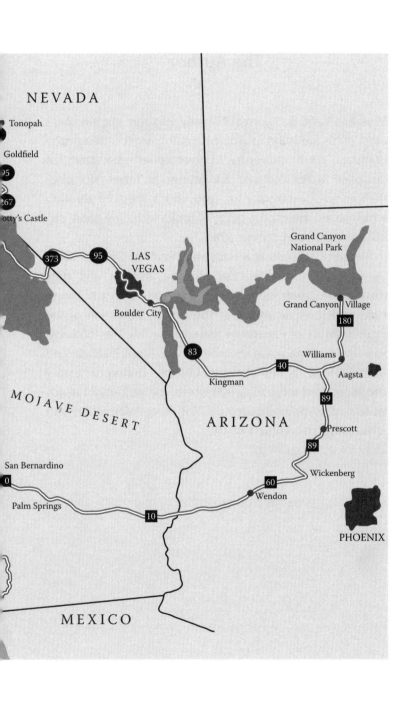

The Author

Mark Brennand was born in Grimsby, England, but has spent most of his life living in Wolverhampton. He is a Geography graduate (Hull University, University of Maryland), a discipline which fostered an interest in travel. His blog, thebrennandpost.blog.co.uk provides a medium through which he airs views on a range of topics including sport, art-house cinema and current affairs.

He met Catherine at a Halloween Party in October 1986. He was a Ghostbuster, she Morticia Addams and they married two years later. In 1991 Catherine won the Young Painter of the Year Award at the Annual Exhibition of the Royal Institute of Painters in Watercolour (RI). The following year she became a full member of the Royal Institute and from 2001 was a member of its Council. During her career she completed more than 900 works, the majority of which were sold to private collectors. For more information visit www.catherinebrennand.co.uk.

They have two children.

Acknowledgements

My mum, Barbara, for her unstinting support in looking after the boys when I needed a break, ditto John & Gill (Catherine's mum and dad). John Lenanton, Bryan Gideon and John and Judy Wilson for their generosity in looking after us during our visit to California. Anne Wright; for giving me the confidence to proceed to publication.

"Any fool can write a novel, but it
takes real genius to sell it"

J G Ballard

Tonopah, Nv

"Are you from Ingerland?" enquired the plump woman sitting at the table opposite.

"Yes" I replied prompting a smile on her round face that she had rightly recognised our accent. "I thought so" she continued "It was the way your boys said 'corn dog' whilst ordering their food."

We were in the dining room of the Ramada Inn, Tonopah Nv. For some time this woman had been making admiring glances at my two, who were sitting quietly reading their books, whilst she had been reprimanding her teenage daughter over some trivial misdemeanour.

"Where are you from?" she asked.

"A town called Wolverhampton" which as expected brought the usual blank expression. So I continued "It's about 20 minutes north of Birmingham" and I pointed to a huge sign over the server which read "Birmingham Industry". How such a sign should find its way into the unlikely setting of a hotel in this rustbelt of a Nevadan mining town was a mystery. Just below it was sited another link to Birmingham in the form of an old advert for Cadbury's Chocolate whose factory is located there. For a moment I wondered if Tonopah was harbouring some secretive link to England's second city.

"Ahh" she nodded although I wasn't convinced that she was any the wiser. She continued "our daughter has just spent part of this year studying in Cambridge." Her daughter turned and beamed.

For a moment I thought that she had been one of the

fortunate few to attend Britain's top University but then thought that she didn't look old enough. "That's a nice town" I offered "Good university" and then for some inexplicable reason I tried to paint a visual picture of where it was in relation to Wolverhampton. "It's about 120 miles from where we live. Not very far but then nowhere is very far in England".

"She wants to go back to study in England when she finishes at High School. She's thinking about going to Nottingham Trent University."

"That's another nice town" I ventured sounding more and more like a representative for the UK tourist board. Then again anything is a nice town when compared to Wolverhampton. In a pop chart of towns and cities of England, Wolverhampton would struggle to break into the top 100. It is more Trenton NJ than Boston Ma.

"Where have you come from today?" I asked shifting the focus.

"We've driven up from Las Vegas. We are then heading up to Lake Tahoe for a few days".

"You live in Vegas?" I asked, prompting a look which said "pull-lease". Her voice however carried none of the apparent opprobrium. "No we are from LA. We live below the H in Hollywood. You might have seen it when you flew in".

"I looked for it I have to say but couldn't see it. Perhaps we were on the wrong side of the plane", at which point the waitress brought their bill.

With impeccable timing her husband returned from a break in the casino, no doubt lighter in terms of dollars than when he had left. "Are we set?" he asked and receiving a nod the four of them prepared to leave. "Well it's been nice meeting you and I hope you have a good time on your travels". "You too" I said and they departed.

Two and a half years ago we too had been a four. That was until my wife Catherine had tragically died, aged 44, of breast cancer. It was day five of our western adventure. We had reached Tonopah, the kind of place you only visit because it's half way to somewhere else. The kind of place you can claim, with some certainty, to being alone in having visited.

Sunday 10th August 2008 – Wolverhampton, UK

7.30am

I wake to the cry of a magpie that roosts under the eaves of our house in the quiet suburban oasis of Newbridge, two miles from Wolverhampton town centre. As he flies off, the raucous cackle is replaced by the monotonous cooing of a distant wood pigeon. They are voracious, destructive birds and I'd like to cull them, but have neither the means nor the guts to do so.

I get up to go for a pee. The boys are asleep in their bunks but I choose not to wake them. They will need all the rest they can get. For today we are going to California.

Since booking the flight in January the big day has hurtled towards us, foreshortened by a combination of advancing years and parental responsibilities. I'm apprehensive. The challenge of Heathrow, the length of the flight, American Customs, the driving once we get there and the length of our break. Three weeks. It's twenty years since I last went away for three weeks. And of that occasion by week two, I was ready for home. It's not however the duration that is my main concern. Will it be a break, a time to relax, or a daily slog of hotels, sight-seeing and driving? … driving across mile upon mile of desolate desert. From afar I feared the latter.

Preparations began earlier in the week with a start on the packing. Packing. A challenge for one, let alone three. The odds on warm dry weather were high, but my belt and braces approach appears excessive. Do I really need all this kit? Later, on the plane, I would read an article in the In Flight magazine and an interview with a New Zealand film producer whose tip on packing went something like: "Pack your bag. Go away for 20 minutes. Return and halve your belongings. Go away again. Return in another 20 minutes and halve them again." If only I'd read it earlier.

As the day unfolds it becomes apparent that my apprehension is misplaced. The motorway is clear and we have no trouble finding our long stay car park, close to Heathrow. I'd stayed here before when Catherine and I visited Malta to research subjects for what would subsequently be a sell-out exhibition of her paintings. Although two years ago, I remembered that it was both easy to find and well placed for the airport. I like familiarity.

Our arrival at Q Park could not have been better timed for within minutes a shuttle bus takes us straight to Terminal 2. From outside it projects the tired visage of a facility from a by-gone era. Hardly surprising therefore that during the last twelve months Heathrow has been something of a political football. (see panel below).

We find our check in desk easily. The queue is long but it keeps moving and as it does I engage in some people watching. Australian over there, Russian behind us, NZ to a left, English two ahead. Not that many Americans, mind. And before we know it we are being summoned to check in our baggage. Choosing to fly on a Sunday is turning out to be a good decision as our experience is at odds with the doomsayers who think the airport a basket case.

Heathrow Airport

For Heathrow the year 2008 was an Annus Horribilis. Tagged "The world's busiest international airport" it achieves this feat from just two overstretched runways. Aware of its limitation and keen to promote economic growth ahead of a cod commitment to saving the environment, in 2007 the Government commissioned an enquiry into the construction of a third runway. Surrounded as it is by large areas of residential housing it did not take long for the ire of local resident to be raised. Their objections culminated the following May, with a huge protest opposing the move and questions raised in Parliament. Caught in the crossfire, Heathrow needed positive news and looked to the opening of its state of art Terminal Five to provide it. On 27th March 2007 the Terminal was officially opened by the Queen. But joy soon turned to anger as the baggage handling system collapsed. Legion was the luggage that went astray prompting unrestrained fury from those caught up in the carnage. As chaos reigned flights were cancelled in what was hailed as a metaphor of our national decline. We like nothing more than self flagellation. Predictably the press had a field day with Heathrow's stock slumping to that of a pariah state. And yet out of this car crash has a phoenix risen. Six months on and Heathrow appears to be functioning perfectly well. Given the constraints placed upon it, this is a minor miracle. But whether it fits the bill for a glorious future, remains in question.

So, the anticipated chaos at Heathrow had not arisen. The flight too was a doddle. We were travelling Cattle Class. What a sleight on the way most of us have to travel. It's clearly not Business Class but it's hardly slumming it. And our Air New Zealand Jumbo was brand spanking new with upholstery unsullied by hours of use and television screens in every seat back. The boys had brought their faithful Nintendos, perfect I thought for whiling away endless hours of inactivity. Yet the presence of the seat back TVs soon rendered them redundant. In a sign of the generational gap they immediately grasped the rudiments of the control unit, flicking through the options for films, games and music before settling on the crass *Austin Powers and the Gold Member*. I'm not entirely sure I approved.

Eventually I too succumb to the need for entertainment, choosing *Kung Fu Panda* which proved humorously diverting.

Whilst the seat back TVs were a real boon, I couldn't help but think that something was missing. There used to be a time when everyone watched the same film on a large screen attached to one of the bulkheads and when the film had finished you either continued to listen to the music or, more commonly, removed your earphones and had a conversation with the person next to you. Sadly, no longer.

Since anything could be watched at any time almost to a man everybody wore earphones and gawped at their screens. Even announcements from the cockpit informing us that "if you look out of the right hand side of the aircraft you can see what used to be Greenland before planes like this created greenhouse gases, global warming and thus caused it to melt…." are a thing of the past. Merely select the page which tells you about the flight and you have instant access to your exact position, height, airspeed, km travelled, km to travel, eta, temperature at destination, whether Leanne will be part of your welcoming party, what shoes she is wearing and if she's decided to put her hair up or not. Thus, apart from the occasional Basil Fawlty induced snigger, noise was there none. Cocooned as we were in our little iPod world, it was like a living morgue.

For Brits one of the great joys of flight is the experience of arriving at a destination where the temperature is warmer than that which has been left. In this instance, given how cold and wet the summer had been, not difficult. It was thus with a sense of anticipation that, eleven hours after our departure, we were exiting the plane with the prospect of warm air none too distant. However as we entered Terminal 2 of LAX Arrivals we now found ourselves facing the prospect of a tough inquisition at the hands of US Customs. Which is where the day's second pronouncement, was soon discredited.

I'd been warned to expect a rough ride. "US Customs is awful. It will take you at least an hour to get through. Whatever you do don't cross the yellow line, don't make eye contact or conversation and don't smile. They are humourless".

Right. Prepare to behave.

Like sheep being corralled into a dip, we are led by those temporary lane stands along a circuitous trail. As at Heathrow however things were quiet and it appeared that we were the only flight alighting at that time. And with so many staff on duty within 10 minutes we were being summoned to a Customs Officer. He smiled and by turn looked at each of our passports whilst calling out our names. "Only three?" he asked and then turning to Tom, "Where's your mom?" almost as if she might be held up in the toilet. "She's dead" I said with finality. The question is rarely asked but when it is there is no value hiding behind euphemism.

Well trained or not he showed few outward signs of embarrassment. "You here for business, or pleasure?" "Pleasure … we hope" I said breaking the rule about no conversation. Then apropos of nothing he started telling us about how he had come to America from Vietnam some seven years ago and that he'd worked hard, kept his nose clean and had worked his way up to his current position within the Immigration Service. Why he should think that we might be interested I don't know but I smiled and nodded politely as one does when in the presence of someone in authority. He then took our fingerprints and what looked like an image of my iris. And that was it. We were through. "Y'all have a good holiday".

"Thank you" I said and off we went to collect our bags.

We may criticise London Heathrow but Terminal 2 of LAX falls some way short of what one might expect of the world's only superpower. Pokey and rather seedy were two initial impressions. But we had not travelled all this way to sit in an arrivals lounge. Outside onto the sidewalk, where a constant stream of taxis and cars are pulling up. The air carried that unmistakable whiff of unleaded petrol. But what did I care? It was sensually warm and, more importantly, we had arrived.

Monday 10th August 2008 – Costa Mesa, Ca

A day to relax and regain a sense of equilibrium.

Last night John had arranged for us to be collected by Shuttle bus from the airport and this took us to his home in Costa Mesa where he has lived for the last 34 years. Denied the aid of satellite navigation the driver had to rely on that relic of a by-gone era – an A–Z – to find John's house. In the dark, no easy task.

After a number of wrong turns we eventually arrived and as the taxi pulled up out came John and Bryan to greet us. It was great to see them and we shook hands and hugged one another.

The boys were on their last legs, desperate for sleep but the offer of food and some gentle encouragement ensured that we kept them awake until the last possible moment. I was not long in following them, John kindly giving over his bedroom.

Not surprisingly my sleep was disrupted by the change in time zones and by 6.30am I was wide awake. John's bedroom adjoins a small courtyard and it's not long before I'm sitting outside surrounded by terracotta pots containing orange and lemon trees and borders filled with lavender and dwarf rosemary. It's a little slice of Tuscany and only the sun is missing, unable to break through a thick layer of cloud.

I am soon joined by John complete with a pot of Fortnum and Mason's Breakfast tea. He may have lived here for many years but has lost none of his English roots. I had known him since the mid seventies when he and his French wife

The first of many fabulous breakfasts.

MBrownand.

Jacqui were in the early stages of establishing a seemingly glamorous life as émigrés in California.

We caught up with our respective news and having done so I roused the boys who were dozing. A bribe of croissants and petit pain for breakfast, gets them moving.

The day's priority was to collect the hire car that I'd pre-booked over the internet with Thrifty. John Wayne Airport appeared to be their nearest location but it proved not that easy to find. (It helps before departing to key in the correct Zip Code on Yahoo Maps) Furthermore it was underground and thus geared more to airline travellers.

That said the sales rep was accommodating his stock rising as he notes that we are from Wolverhampton and tells me that he follows Wolverhampton Wanderers. We discussed their prospects for the season ahead before he pointed outside to a black Dodge Caliber which in the subterranean half light looked very black indeed. A cursory check of the bodywork confirmed that all looked fine and that was it. OK it might not have been the highest spec car in the world but what it did have was air conditioning, a cd player and that all important accessory luminous cup holders. More fundamental than any of these extras however, was its pedigree. It was a Dodge – the make of car which, in 1981 as a post grad student at the University of Maryland, became the first vehicle I ever owned. I felt at home.

By the early afternoon the temperature had reached an uncomfortable 30°C. To escape the heat, John suggested that we go to the beach at Crystal Cove, just south of Coruna Del Mar. The journey was all rather depressing. When last here, Newport was hemmed in by the physical presence of Newport Bay, Balboa Island being its most southerly point. From there Corona Del Mar was a separate community beyond which was Laguna Beach similarly detached.

No longer.

Now, as we drove south along Newport Coast Drive, (a road that had not been here twenty years ago), the landscape was dominated by mile upon mile of suburban sprawl. In Britain, with its lack of space, strict planning laws still provide a modest curb on development. But here, in this developer's gold mine, there appeared none. John reckoned that most of the houses were in the $1m bracket. "Where do all these people work?" I pondered, since this part of Southern California is not noted for its industry. "They can't all be lawyers, surely?"

Descending a winding highway we pass the Greco Roman entrance to Pelican Hills, one of these sprawling developments. Opposite, in marked contrast, is the modest entrance to Crystal Cove. John is a regular visitor but this doesn't prevent the ranger from insisting that she view his pass. "I come here three times a week yet she always stops me" he said with a hint of irritation.

From our raised vantage we can see the grey outline of Santa Catalina Island and, closer to shore, a small flotilla of yachts sails spread taut in the perfect breeze. To get to the beach you walk through an area of dry scrub before descending a steep tarmacadam path. Below, gathered around the lifeguard station are a gaggle of folk mainly couples and families with young children, enjoying the sun. Every now and again the cry of a child breaks the calm as they jump to avoid a breaking wave.

We need to work off our lunch so walk down to Crystal Cove proper, a bohemian enclave of gentrified beach huts.

It is the holiday season and there are lots of families here drawn by the proximity of the amenities provided by a restaurant and board hire outlet. Many children are in the sea enjoying the surf and practising on their body boards, waiting for a wave to break and start its advance up the sand before jumping onto them to slide over the thin layer of water like a car aquaplaning. My two are soon stripped off and ready for battle. You get a true sense of the size of the Pacific when, on even the most benign of days, the waves are bigger than any that they had previously experienced. They have a great time playing in the surf and more than once are turned and spun by the strength of the surf.

MBrennand

From the calm of my towel I observe the goings on. It's a sociable place. Families chilling out under parasols, a couple playing beach tennis and all the while a constant passage of folk, mainly pairs, chatting animatedly as they walk the length of the beach. Much the same as would happen on any beach anywhere in the world.

When we finally call time my two are, understandably, reluctant to leave. But any sense of disappointment is soon allayed as we arrive home to find Bryan preparing the evening meal. "What joy" I think, "to be spared the daily grind of cooking and washing up".

Tuesday 12th August – Disneyland

If you come to Los Angeles then a day at Disneyland is a must. Which is what we did today.

Our *Rough Guide* described it thus; "Disneyland is still world renowned as one of the defining hallmarks of American culture, a theme park phenomenon with the emphasis strongly on family fun; while visitors have been known to cruise around Disneyland on LSD, it is not a good idea. The authorities take a dim view of anything remotely antisocial, and anyone acting out of order will be thrown out. In any case, the place is surreal enough without the need for mind expanding drugs." I had been before but it didn't numb the sense of enjoyment. In fact you would have to be something of an old curmudgeon not to appreciate its charms. Plastic and superficial it may be, but it creates a sense of pure enjoyment that is hard to beat. My two had a marvellous time as we sampled all the major rides, Space Mountain and Indiana Jones getting top billing. For me it's The Pirates of the Caribbean which, twenty years on, had lost none of its charm.

By 5.30pm it was time to head home, back along Harbour Blvd. Boys satiated. Dad ready for a cup of tea.

Wednesday 13th August

Today marked the start of our travels proper and heeding the advice of the NZ film producer, I halved the number of clothes to take with us. They can now fit in to a single suitcase, albeit a large one.

Before we leave there is time to read the *New York Times*, John directing me to a leader penned by Thomas Friedman. "He should be advising the government" he says. Light lunch, al fresco and by 1.30pm it's time to go. We are taking two cars and in order to benefit from the 2 Persons or More Lane Tom went with John, Jack with me.

Our destination is Ojai, where John and Judy Wilson live. Nestling in the foothills of the Los Padres mountains, it is a favoured resort of LA jet setters and celebrities. Not that John and Judy would regard themselves as either.

Our route took us north on Interstate 405 where I encouraged Jack to start recording brief snippets of the journey on our camcorder. One of those things that begins with the best of intentions only to become something of a chore. And when you get home never to be watched. Before long Santa Monica is reached and here we leave the freeway and head north along the Pacific Coast Highway.

Malibu came and went without really registering on our conscience. It is a strange linear place, with a reputation that exceeds the bland façade of wooden clad buildings and garage doors that greet one.

Out passed the imposing presence of Pepperdine University, before the road clings by its fingernails to the side of the Point Mugu range. Eventually the landscape flattens out and we enter the fertile faming land of the Oxnard Plain. Ahead lay mile upon mile of prime agricultural land famous for its strawberries and lima beans. In the fields on either side were gangs of Mexican farmhands either operating machinery or tending to crops. Without Mexicans California's economy would collapse and here was clear proof. Drawing to a stop at a level crossing I noticed John in the car ahead, gesticulating to Tom to take a look at the surroundings. I didn't know it at the time but he had spent nearly the whole of the journey playing a game called Spectrobe on his Nintendo. I acknowledge that it offers a challenge but not to the exclusion of all.

From Oxnard it was but a short journey to Ventura, where a sign on the outskirts indicated a population of some 180,000. Small by Californian standards, large if you compare it to England. Larger for instance than either Blackburn or Preston, two famous Lancashire mill towns. Such things put America's vast size into perspective.

Reaching Ventura our route then headed north into the Los Padres Mountains and Ojai where John and Judy live in a secluded gated community. So secluded in fact that we missed the entrance. We needed to call security to get the gate opened and once onto the estate I found it all bewildering. Every house was enormous and each in turn surrounded by a large garden all carefully laid out and beautifully manicured. John and Judy's Spanish style villa was no less impressive.

A bright light snuffed out

It was fourteen years since we had met. Back then our time together had been confined to a round of golf and an evening meal with friends. In the short time together we had established a clear rapport and during the ensuing years had maintained contact by mail and through interest in Catherine's work as a watercolour artist. John and Judy had bought four of her works and were convinced that her paintings would appeal to the local populace. Thus did Judy raise the notion of getting Catherine to exhibit at a gallery in Santa Barbara. To do this would require a visit to conduct the research, a process which involved walking tours of towns and cities taking photographs of buildings. Once processed they were sequenced chronologically before selecting those that would make suitable subjects to paint. If she had a large exhibition Catherine would pick around eighteen images and, having done so, this would be followed by three months of intensive painting. She could work quickly with six works on the go at any one time. Her studio occupied a bedroom at home which meant that, when the boys were small, she could combine child care with her work. It was a testament to both her drive and talent that, during this period, she made a living solely from her art.

By the January of 2002 Jack was in the Infants and Tom was ready to go to nursery school. A milestone marking the end of that intensive period of child care had been reached. And with it more time to paint. Catherine's reputation grew and I too prospered in my role as a School Inspector. Life at that particular time was good.

A high point came in May with a week staying in a small Umbrian villa. Free from the children (who were cared for by Catherine's mum and dad) we had time to ourselves and, when not relaxing by the pool, embarked on a series of visits to Assissi, Gubbio, Cortona and Perugia. It was a magical time and we returned refreshed and looking forward with optimism.

However as is often the case, life has a capacity to kick you when least expected. Unbeknown to me, for some time Catherine had been aware of a lump in her left breast. Never one to worry she had chosen to ignore it but on the evening of Wednesday 17th July, just as she was getting ready for bed, she turned to me and said "That doesn't feel very good. I'll have to go and get it checked out first thing tomorrow." Even now, these words make me go cold.

Within two days she'd been referred to New Cross Hospital for a mammogram and biopsy. I was working in my office at home when she returned. Although physically small she was a tough little character and it was therefore all the more disturbing that she should immediately burst into tears. I had never seen her so distressed and all I could think was; what on earth are we facing here? And with that began the most anxious weekend, awaiting the results.

But our discomfort was as nothing when, the following Wednesday, we were summoned to New Cross Hospital for the news. There, in the soulless surroundings of an examination room the hammer blow was struck. She did indeed have breast cancer. I can only surmise that at that very point Catherine must have been in complete turmoil and yet, as the dreadful news sank home, she maintained an outward calm. I felt physically sick.

A further mammogram was immediately arranged to determine the size and location of the tumour and we were then asked "Do you want a lumpectomy or a full mastectomy." Left alone for a short while to make the decision we were as one in choosing the latter. They then added, somewhat scarily, that they wouldn't know whether the cancer had infected any other organs until they'd completed the operation. All I could think was "Please tell me that this isn't happening".

So began life, living with cancer, a state of constant fear, of never knowing the full extent of the threat with no apparent means of escape. It is this fear of the unknown that is the most debilitating aspect of the disease as phrases such as, "We won't know the state of things until we've had the results of the scan" or "We'll have a better idea when we've got the results of your blood test" become part of the lexicon of a new and anxious life.

It seemed like an eternity before she had her operation on Monday 19th August. Her surgeon, Dr Matey, did a remarkable job. Dealing with the knowledge that she had cancer was hard enough and it was therefore vital that she retain physical self esteem. The boob job, to put it crudely, did the trick.

From the outset, rather than put her life on hold by seeking a miracle cure, Catherine placed total faith in the team at the Deansley Centre, the new cancer treatment unit at New Cross Hospital in Wolverhampton. Led by the taciturn Dr Mehra, he negotiated the fine line between telling it as it was and maintaining morale. He became a trusted aid as did all those who would subsequently look after her.

In the year following her mastectomy life was as close to normal as it could possibly be, although for Catherine, the effects of an eight month course of chemotherapy and radiotherapy knocked even her sunny view of life. It was remarkable how she kept things going and particularly her painting. One might even say that the dreadful news instilled in her a renewed determination to make her mark. Despite the endless round of check-ups, treatment and remission, from September 2002, she produced some of her most notable work.

The window of nomality – it's a relative term – lasted around 18 months. By the May of 2004 she was experiencing back pain and it wasn't long before those dreaded scans confirmed our worst fears. The cancer had spread to her spine. Good news and cancer are rare bed fellows. Stable is about the best one can hope for. Time and again she would return from yet another scan, give me the news in the most sensitive way and then with implacable pluck utter "Well I'm still here. They are developing new treatments all the time and I'll just have to get on with it". And with that she'd disappear to her studio.

This remarkable spirit was Catherine's way of protecting us all from the dark side of cancer and for the most part it worked. For there were many happy times during her post cancer diagnosis. It was just that when the bad news arose the consequences were so serious that, looking back, they simply overwhelmed all that was good.

And, as if to prove the point, in the June of 2005 scans showed that the cancer had now spread to her liver. At the time Catherine kept this from me, knowing that I would worry unduly and it was only when a second course of chemotherapy was scheduled to start in August that she had to come clean. But the way in which she told me was so matter of fact that one might think she was suffering from a minor ailment.

Catherine was an occasional diarist. She would start with the best of intentions only to find daily journal entries a chore. There would therefore be no John Diamond style account of living with cancer but every now and again she did find time to record her thoughts;

31st August 2005

Just finished first batch of Taxotere — chemo for my liver. Must be grim stuff because I have had to have my blood pressure monitored. I had the Cold Cap again, after chopping my hair off last night. Let's hope it works! Can't believe I'm back with this again. Still I've had 2½ years free of chemotherapy and I'm still pretty fit.

Can't even think what the date is ... Wednesday 7th September. I had chemo last Wednesday and it's been a bit of a rollercoaster lately. Since last week I've not really felt sick, but very dizzy and washed out. Mum and Dad brought the boys back on Saturday and Dad when went back to Wales to do some work on his caravan club articles while Mum stayed here. Boys back at school on Monday and oblivious to everything! It's been lovely weather so we've done lots of sitting outside and a bit of piano duets each day. It's been very, very strange not to feel particularly unwell but so weak and feeble. I've sat at my studio table to label my Tuscany photographs but really didn't feel up to much. It's very different really from last time when I felt unwell and could fight through it with a bit of painting. This time I can't get my head together and my arms and legs feel twitchy.

Still, things are so much more simple with both the boys now at school and able to get themselves up. They are really quite independent and can get down to Kerry's on their own so I don't even have to get dressed.

Mark is also home much more and not away on Ofsted inspections at all this term. So far. The work situation is so much better for him really, with the regular two days a week at Taxrale

15th September 2005 · Thursday
Another J-TOX! It's been a real roller coaster of a cycle with my neutropenia being so dramatically low. Now it's my haemoglobin levels so low that I'll have to have a blood transfusion on Monday (hopefully!) I do feel RATHER washed out and headachey and they reckon that's why. Another blood test now and then I can pop into town on the way home, it's been AGES since I've been allowed out and I've a cheque from the Shell House to pay in "Rice Wine Shop, Soho" a v. nice small painting. But only the second they've sold after out of 12. Must think about how I could ... ??

Monday 19th September

· Newcross again, having a blood transfusion. At least the cannula's in my left hand so I can write this. I am so enjoying "Author, Author" by David Lodge about Henry James, I don't want to race through it too soon! I have only recently ~~read~~ read "The Master" by Colm Toibin and a year before had Joan Aiken's book "Lamb House" out of the library as a talking book. It occurs to me that I've read more ~~books~~ books ABOUT Henry James than actually read books BY him. Mind you he is hard work. I really enjoyed "The Aspern Papers" and "The Turn of the Screw." But actually I don't think I read "Portrait of a Lady" I listened to it as a Radio 4 Classic Serial or maybe it was Women's Hour. Must get "Daisy Miller."

WORK — Spent ages doing Open Day Invitations over the weekend. Can't believe how many there are this year — it must be all the Demos and workshops I've done this past 18 months — but there must be 200+. Will have to get Mark to collect from the Galleries this year. It will be tricky because I've no new work to give them

because I've been flat out working on the Malta pictures. Only 5 more to complete. Maybe I could fit in a few small pictures before I get started on my R1 set. And I need to offer some work to Gideon Baunton.... John Guthrie's commission ... Pat Vella's commission ... Thomas Pink for the Lesters (nearly finished) Otherwise nothing to do!!

1. PHOTOCOPYING — Open Day Invitations + RSVP cards
   ⎰ Mdina, last Malta picture

2. Invitations, write and send

3. I. Vittoriosa II. Mdina, Palazzo Falzonne
   III. St. Paul's Shipwreck Church* IV. ADC Valletta
   V. Tall Green Valletta + window boxes

4. *Extra Photographs for Christmas card

5. Sketches of Tuscan Landscapes: Guthries
   + PHOTOCOPY

10. Helen Thomas commission !!

6. Finish Thomas Pink for Open Day (+ frame) Lesters.

7. <u>TUSCANY SKETCHES</u>: Small Pieces
   1. Hew Alex x 4   2. Shell House x 4 *first choice*
   3. LB6 x 4   * 4. Gideon Bainton
  * 5. R1 x 3 (already 3 London Sketches)

is she really interested?!

8. Any odd pictures started complete for Open Day
9. Ikea for frames (+ clip frames)

Oh well, I suppose it's good to keep busy.!!
Now that my chemotherapy is underway, I am very
philosophical about the whole thing. Also it's a great
excuse for not getting things done!

Monday : 12.15 Dr. Mehra	24 SAT .
Tuesday : Sainsburys. Mark went	25 SUN : Durrants "D8"
Wednesday 11am CHEMO eve. Yoga	Mon 26.
Thursday :	Tues 27.
Friday :	Wed 28.
	Thurs 29 J. Tox
	Fri 30 Pat Vella

<u>WED 21st</u>

Back at NewCross for 2nd session of Taxotere chemo.
Actually, looking back at my last list I've done really
well and completed several things — Photocopying;
the Invitations; the Mdina drawing already stretched
and the Painting "168 Merchants St (ADC) Valletta"
So now, just 4 more pictures to finish, show them to Pat Vella
and then send them.
Had a row with Mark about new work for galleries. We
agreed that Gideon Bainton is the priority, and his left overs
will be OK for the R1. The Open Day is the next priority. Must
list all work in Galleries, do some "swaps" and explain how I
must re-use frames (to explain taking away work)

On the way home: <u>Pak Continental</u> : ground almonds, rice
     plenty spice pastes. PEARS.
  Penn : <u>Music 2000</u>, Jack's music for Brass butter • eggs.

New List <u>Malta</u> 1. Mdina, Palazzo Fallzonn · started drawing
          2. Tall thin, green & blue Valletta · painting well on
          3. Vittoriosa, Vittoriosa · painting half way
          4. St. Paul's Shipwreck church · painting halfway

Make Pear tart for Durrants on Sunday + flowers
(·Healthy curry for Ann- chicken balti ?
Home grown produce? Lettuce & Runner beans.

THURS 29 Sept 2005

Urg, such a FOUL taste in my mouth! And sore too.
An ache at the top of my pelvis, that makes me move like a
Right Old Woman! Still, haven't had the desperate
DIZZY tiredness of Cycle 1 and also the aches and pains
in my legs. Weird. Keeping a constant watch on my
temperature — I should be neutropenic now (Day 9)
What's been good about this Cycle is that I've been able
to keep on working and now only have 1 Malta
painting to complete!! Can you believe it? St. Paul's
Shipwreck Church in Valletta.   Been very, very sensible today.
As it's Cleaning Day, I did the usual changing towels
etc, but altho' it's been sunny I used the Dryer, got
everything dry quickly to put back on the beds and bathroom.
Now I'm sitting in the car while Jack and Tom go swimming.
They have to go in the Male Changing Room now, so I can't
supervise their showers/changing etc and I don't think the
claustrophobic humid atmosphere of the pool is ideal for
my health situation. SO I've BRIBED them! Yes! Two
£5.00 notes are sitting on my dashboard waiting to give
them, for being diligent and showering properly. Am I mad?
when I can't see what they're up to? Well I don't know
what else to do. They're really playing me up at the
moment, particularly Jack. He's morose and sulky
and not his usual willing cheerful self.. Tom is always

more challenging, but lately just a pain all the time. They're a catalogue of toys, and have picked all they want. Great I thought! Incentive! But no, it's not worked at all. They're got worse and worse and only two stars have appeared on the chart since Saturday when we set up the situation again. Perhaps these fivers, as Solid Currency, will focus their minds more.

Two days later Catherine finished the final painting for the Malta Show.

MONDAY 3rd OCT
Waiting for J. Tex. Symptoms ⊂ v. bad constipation
bad lower back pain
horrible taste in mouth
"burn" on R. hand

WOW! Actually
finished Malta pictures on Friday. Feel rather flat about the whole thing. But 'St. Paul's' is a good painting and the last set are as good as any of the others. My favourites are the shops 'Royal Pharmacy' "ADC" and "Joseph Butesill" I do hope they get their act together and sort out a gallery and dates for me.

when I get back must sort out pictures to photograph. I've got this Demo and have nearly got my drawings ready for it too, already. It's just wonderful to be working on pictures that aren't Malta without FEELING GUILTY ABOUT IT!!

It was typical of Catherine to be so positive. But there were also many days when she brought low by the brutality of the treatment and the never-ending round of hospital appointments. It seemed as if she spent half her life at the Deansley Centre.

Denied the time to paint became an experience more incapacitating than the treatment. Increasingly bitter about the unfairness of her circumstance and adversely affected by the concoction of drugs that she was taking, her outbursts became more frequent. To my everlasting regret I selfishly viewed these as a personal sleight, when all that she sought was a sympathetic ear. I would bridle and in no time at all we would be at loggerheads, shouting angrily at one another. Things came to a head one evening when, following tea, we fell out over an issue so trivial that I cannot remember it. As angry insults bounced around the house, it was only when Jack started to cry and with a plaintiff "mum … dad … please stop", that I recognised the depth to which I had sunk. It would mark a watershed.

Looking back at that time I recognise that, prior to cancer, we had argued very rarely. Yet now, faced with the strains of coping with an ordeal whose dreadful endgame was becoming ever more apparent, we had nowhere to go. It was nobody's fault. My beautiful wife was dying. Our blessed life was collapsing.

Despite the awful strain, in 2005 Catherine still managed to complete 36 paintings for an exhibition in Malta. It would be her first and only One Woman Show and was held over the weekend of the 17th/18th February 2006. I considered these works to be some of the best she had ever done and my confidence was confirmed when, within two days, the exhibition had all but sold out. On the morning of Saturday 18th a day after the Private View, she wrote;

Sat 19th Feb'

In Valletta, waiting for my baguette at Eddie's Café Regina "a Snack in the heart of the city". Sadly the service is Not Good. Still, it's lovely to be able to sit outside in February, it's not as warm as yesterday but very pleasant. Also not bad a feeling having sold 33 out of 36 paintings! The Private View was a terrific event, very well organised and masses and masses of people. I talked all evening and met loads of really interesting and complementary — very complementary people. Very flattering speeches by the ex-president and Nicholas de Piro. The latter, we met last time and he showed us round his palace in Valletta. I sat next to him at the supper and his wife Frances (known as 'Ding') They were both supper company and I got given Nicky's book as well as gorgeous flowers. The Bolognas are now getting on with their lives — being "exhausted" and I won't see them again. But they insisted on paying my hotel bill and dinner on Thursday, so they have been very generous. It's just a different style and I suppose I'll just have to get used to it, because they're determined to repeat the exercise because it's been so successful, but I'll will have to be 2007. I must do some paintings of Malta in the meantime — for the Open Day for example as so many of Barbara's cronies have Maltese connections.

By this time she had just finished her second course of chemotherapy and was looking forward with renewed optimism. Despite the brave front, there were more and more days when she was in pain. In my heart I knew that she was far from well, and began to steel myself to the awful thought that she might not survive the year.

Now, more than ever, she needed something to look forward to. Returning from Malta I booked for us all to go to California in August, the intention being that she could carry out the research for Judy's exhibition.

But in April things took another turn for the worse. Her eyes had started to move out of sync, causing double vision. As ever she didn't worry unduly but it clearly concerned her oncologist, Dr Mehra. He knew it to be a possible sign that a tumour had formed in her brain. But, until it could be confirmed, he kept his thoughts to himself. There followed a frantic round of scans which were inconclusive. We took this as a positive, particularly since we had arranged to fly out to France over the Easter holidays to stay with Catherine's cousins. Understandably Dr Mehra was reluctant to let her go but eventually relented when faced by her enthusiasm and pluck. Thus on Friday 14th April, two days after I had departed with the boys, she found herself at Birmingham Airport waiting to join us;

FRIDAY 14th APRIL · Paid £3·15 for coffee + pastry
Here I am at B'ham Airport — need to keep a
record of my drugs consumption! Have a terrible
choc croissant + latte with 3 × DEX at around 8am.
But I do feel much less sick. I had 250ml of Octomorph
at 6am so I'm allowed another spoonful now but I'm
trying to eke it out a bit. If I wait 'til 9.30 I can make
its 'til Bergerac 1·30pm Brit time. I'll in the lounge and
haven't got a gate No. yet.

All rather in a dream world with the double vision and
I feel as rough as when I've had chemotherapy. Gave all
the gory details to the taxi driver who was 15 minutes
late. It is so annoying how they say "Oh there's plenty of
time" and "not to worry"! They don't seem to see that if
they've agreed to pick you up at 6·30 that's when you want
to be picked up because you don't want to be rushed
to the station last minute. Oh well. I've not missed a train
yet, but that isn't the point, when they've agreed to pick you
up at 6·30.
Might have a wander around the shops for a minute then
have my spoonful!

PROJECTS

1. Phone Alaine Bologna + send 2 Malta Commissions!
2. Put Guthrie pictures in frames
3. Collect framing and deliver Helen Thomas's pictures
4. Invoice Helen Thomas and copy to Jim Ireland
5. Phone Bobbie at LBG to deliver her pictures
6. Debra Grech paintings   a) finish them
                            b) framing c) deliver
                                        (Kim Laws?)

7. ANDY & KATE SPEAR

They were to be her last recorded words.

Our French sojourn was at once the happiest, yet saddest five days of my life. Free of the boys for prolonged periods, we had time to ourselves and, as we had always done, just talked and talked. And as we did, so for the first time since contracting this awful disease, Catherine finally acknowledged that it was getting the better of her. Steadfast throughout, with an optimism that made me believe she would win through, to hear her now resigned to a premature death was truly heartbreaking.

Within days of our return to England a third scan confirmed that a tumour had indeed formed in her brain. In a last desperate effort they tried radiotherapy what I regarded as bordering on cruelty. But it was too late, as a startling decline now took hold. Within days she had slipped into a coma from which she would never emerge.

At 9.45am on Monday 1st May she took her final breath. This selfless, funny, bright and spirited woman was dead. A bright light had indeed been snuffed out.

Monday 1st May 2006

Dear Catherine

It is the first day of summer. The chance to look forward to warmer days, an optimistic day. Yet tragically it is also the day that you, a ceaseless optimist, died.

I had slept poorly and it was all I could do to get up and give the boys their breakfast. Yesterday I'd been given the gut wrenching news that you were dying and were unlikely to live more than 24 hours. In a macabre act I'd been asked to remove all your personal belongings, your engagement and wedding rings. Being in a coma you knew nothing of what was happening but the finality of what I'd been asked to do was heart breaking.

Overnight it came as a relief to learn that you had been moved to the comfortable surroundings of the Deansley Centre, the Cancer Unit at New Cross Hospital. It was at New Cross that you had brought Jack and Tom into the world and it would be New Cross where you would die.

At 9.15am the telephone rang. It was a nurse from the Deansley saying that you were going downhill rapidly. Did I want to come in and sit with you? The question carried with it the implication that I should come in – do the right thing. I can't explain why but I truly didn't want to see you take your final breath. So I stayed at home with your mum and together we occupied ourselves in the practical and somewhat bizarre task of compiling a shopping list.

Twenty minutes later there was another call. It was the same nurse reporting that you had died. I was engulfed by a mixture of relief, great sadness and disbelief. Only two weeks previously we had been wandering around the streets of Bordeaux, researching buildings for your next set of paintings. You were a fully functioning adult and now you are dead.

Putting the telephone down I pulled your mum to one side and told her the news. Inconsolable, we just hugged one another. I then got the boys together. I had forewarned them yesterday that you were dying and I then told them the dreadful news. Tom is only seven and doesn't really understand but it's going to be tough for Jack who is two years older. They too burst into tears and the four of us assembled in a big huddle to comfort one another.

Your mum and I then arranged for them to go and stay with close friends, before we headed to hospital. I have lived 46 years and never set eyes on a dead body. And now here I am staring at you.

I just sat quietly at the end of your bed stroking your feet and repeating that I loved you and that I always had. At times it was as if the bedclothes were moving and you were breathing, or rather I wanted it to be. You are a deathly yellow, your liver having failed. What a terrible terrible waste. I sat with you for twenty minutes just thinking about the wonderful life we have shared. I then kissed you on the forehead and said my final goodbye.

It's just so very very sad.

All my love

M

xxxx

Catherine aged 30

Obituary of Catherine Brennand RI – Watercolour artist

There are some artists who find inspiration and motivation for their work in a variety of sources and themes, and there are others for whom there need only be one. Catherine Brennand's passion was buildings. "Focusing on an individual subject isn't necessarily a bad thing, " she said:

"I cannot imagine ever becoming bored with painting buildings. There are so many architectural styles and every place has its own flavour: Also, as I am particularly interested in the use of light and shadows, the building surface is constantly changing. A good light can make the most mundane of buildings look exciting."

Brennand's work was characterised by its feeling for texture, colour (which was strong, often hot) and composition. – she saw how an interesting doorway or a balcony, out of context, could look almost abstract. But perhaps the most noticeable quality of her work is its sense of atmosphere. In particular she was entranced by shop facades. She did several series including a sequence of Jermyn Street shops in the West End of London. These pictures have a peculiar magic as the reflections in the windows and the glowing lights inside reveal an Aladdin's cave of fine clothes, antique furnishings, jewellery and choice foods

She was born Catherine Bateman in Woking, Surrey in 1961. Her father John Bateman was a journalist with Associated Newspapers and her mother a teacher. When she was still a child the family moved to East Kent and she later attended Dover Grammar School for Girls. On leaving school she went to Bishop Otter College in Chichester to train as a teacher but after three years – and to her parents' alarm – she decided that was the wrong choice for her. She subsequently graduated with a degree in Art and Design from University College, Chichester.

She took a job as a technical and graphic artist with Francis Concrete, a manufacturer of specialist blocks on Ford Airfield, near Chichester. Bateman found that working in the construction industry awakened in her an interest in architecture and she began to paint buildings. Subsequently the firm was taken over and she moved with her job to Wolverhampton.

One night at a Hallowe'en Party she met Mark Brennand, whom she would later marry. Encouraged by him she began to paint regularly and from 1996 worked full time as an artist. She received many and varied commissions which included work for Ivory Gate plc (the Bafta Building), Tarmac, Crown Estates, Staffordshire County Council, Wiltons Restaurant and the New West End Synagogue in London, and the brewery, Eldridge, Pope & Co.

In 1997 she participated in a tour of Israel sponsored jointly by the Linda Blackstone Gallery and the Jewish National Fund for an exhibition the following year celebrating the 50th Anniversary of the state of Israel. The modern buildings along the sea-front of Tel Aviv particularly caught her imagination. Although most of the buildings she painted in Israel were actually white or pale grey, when she recreated them she found inspiration in the colours of the Negev Desert.

She was also drawn to the buildings of Italy, the South of

France and the east coast of the United States. The texture of different materials and surfaces was an important element in her work: the peeling plaster and deep shadows of southern Europe or, in the New England states, the timber cladding and Georgian proportions. Frequently ideas came from the upper storeys of buildings. "Street level is often very ordinary, so I tend to look up quite a lot."

By preference, Brennand worked in watercolour which she enjoyed for its unpredictability and versatility: the medium could stand on its own or be combined with all sorts of other media and techniques. Once back in her studio the photographs she took and sketches she made on site were turned into underlying drawings for her paintings which might be constructed from up to 15 thin layers of superimposed washes of colour.

She said that, whereas the choice of colour was mostly a deliberate and carefully thought-out process, the involvement of textures was largely intuitive. A shelf in front of her working table held all sorts of things used in her work: spray-diffusers, a toothbrush, rollers, screwed up tissue paper, wax crayons and candles (which she used like a batik artist), very fine Japanese papers for glueing onto the paper. Among the artists who influenced her work she named John Piper, Graham Sutherland, Patrick Heron and Mark Rothko.

In 1991 Brennand was awarded the Winsor and Newton Young Painters in Watercolour Award at the Royal Institute of Painters in Watercolous (the RI). The following year she received the Frank Herring Award for the best painting of an architectural subject, after which she became a full member of the institute and in 2001 a member of its council. Her other awards included in 2005 the Matt Bruce Memorial

Prize "for the most outstanding use of light and colour in watercolours".

A prolific artist, she exhibited widely: at the Llewellyn Alexander and Linda Blackstone Galleries in London, the Barnt Green Gallery in Worcester and the Shell House Gallery in Herefordshire, as well as the Royal West of England Academy in Bristol and elsewhere.

Catherine Brennand was an enthusiast for life in all manner of ways. She read avidly, loved letter writing, cooking, Radio 4, fell walking in the Lake District, music, London, architecture, the cinema, buying clothes, good food and conversation.

In March last year she visited Malta where she took around 750 photographs. Despite receiving chemotherapy for breast cancer she spent the summer preparing 40 works for her first one-woman show, which took place in Malta earlier this year. She had remained as much an optimist in her illness as she had in her work. "Painting" she said, "should be good fun."

Simon Fenwick

Catherine Louise Batemen, artist: born Woking Surrey, 11 October 1961; married 1988 Mark Brennand (two sons); died Wolverhampton 1 May 2006

Reprinted by kind permission from The Independent, Obituaries, 3rd August 2006

In the immediate aftermath of Catherine's death I felt enclosed in a dark brooding cloud. I was numb with the shock of what had happened but at the same time relieved that the worry and stress was over. And when I thought that I'd end up feeling guilty. For a while adrenaline carried me along and looking back now I wonder how I got through those first dark months as people returned to their busy lives and I was left to deal with my grief alone.

Adjusting to Catherine's death has been a long, slow and at times contradictory process; the happiness instilled by thinking about her talent, her idiosyncrasies and the great times spent together against a backdrop of grief, anger and disbelief at what has happened. One minute smiling the next crying and all for no apparent reason. And it's the little things that really hurt – her smile, her little handwritten notes, or just a simple "can I get you a cup of tea?" All gone, forever.

But there was never any sense on my part that I would not cope since now, more than ever, the boys needed me. And they in turn have helped by forcing me to focus on the present, rather than dwelling on the past. Almost three years on we are coping remarkably well.

Other things that have helped:

- *Sticking to a routine*
- *Going out regularly with friends*
- *Exercising regularly*
- *Encouraging people to confront the subject rather than skirting around it for fear of offence*

- *Asking friends for help*
- *Keeping a daily journal and recording positive events however small*
- *Having a good cry*
- *Avoiding self pity*

Thursday 17th August 2008

It was an early start. Over dinner the previous evening Judy had offered to take me to the Ojai Spa and Country Club to play a round of golf. I'd played golf in the States on only two previous occasions but never in such prestigious surroundings. Teeing off at 7.50am we had the course to ourselves. And believe me; even if you have never played golf there can be few better ways to spend three and a bit hours than on an empty course in a beautiful setting. Such was the Ojai Spa and Country Club this morning.

Whilst Judy and I strode the fairways John took Jack and Tom to Santa Barbara where they visited the pier, aquarium and Mission and, once the sightseeing had finished, they joined John, Judy and me for lunch at the Country Club.

Before heading home Judy drove us into the centre of Ojai to visit the Post Office. As in the UK they are an endangered entity, email and the growth of competition from alternative carriers eating into their existence. I made sure to stock up with stamps, which was just as well since it would be the last Post Office we would see on our 1,700 mile journey.

More swimming for the boys when we came home whilst I sat down with John, to go through the travel itinerary. Crucially he was going to loan us his Satellite Navigation system for urban navigation. I could see it being vital in helping us locate accommodation in San Francisco and Las Vegas. All the hotel bookings were there together with a wonderful array of Triple AAA maps. We could want for nothing.

Another lovely meal in the evening, chicken fried southern style with fresh corn and a drop of Cabernet Sauvignon from the Napa Valley, all the time listening to the inexorable march of a distant thunderstorm. Rain is alarmingly scarce in these parts and a good downpour was well overdue. It would finally arrive around midnight, dousing everything.

Friday 18th August 2008

Evidence of last night's storm was scant as we woke to a clear blue sky. Standing water was remarkably absent all of it having been absorbed by the bone dry soil. Only in the vegetation, which looked lush and reinvigorated, were there signs of rain.

Having cajoled the boys through their morning wash, I used the remainder of the time before breakfast to pack their belongings. As ever the bedroom was a bombsite, pyjamas and other items of clothing strewn everywhere. There are times when I'm little more than an unpaid domestic.

Cooked breakfast with streaky bacon, so different to that which we are used to back home, was the perfect start and by 10.15 we were ready for the off. It had been lovely to be so well looked after. But it was also lovely to be in charge of our own destiny and to be thinking about what lay ahead on our twelve day adventure. Adventure is perhaps to overstate it, since we were following a well trodden path, the level of risk was low and I was already familiar with many of the places that we would be visiting. However on those previous trips I did not have sole charge of two young boys and in that regard it was a personal challenge.

First objective Santa Barbara, from where we headed up Rte 154 to Solvang. Here we stopped for a comfort break and a brief tour of this ersatz piece of Denmark. For all its pretence Solvang offers an interesting diversion and is well worth visiting. Strange to consider that this had been my third visit, yet never once have I been to Denmark. A comment, perhaps, on the relative draw of our EU neighbour.

Back to the open road. From 154 it was a short jaunt to Rte 101, heading north in the direction of San Luis Obispo. Disturbingly I couldn't remember very much of it.

Consulting John's notes they warned us that when we got to San Luis we needed to keep a wary eye for directions to The Pacific Coast Highway since it was easily missed. Here the help of the boys was vital in providing an extra pair of eyes and it was Jack who first spotted the sign. Getting used to road signage in the States is always a challenge since they tend not to give you much warning of the impending turn off. With owl-like concentration we fixed our gaze on the signs and at the appropriate moment chose what I thought to be the correct exit. Almost immediately we headed back on ourselves. "Oh no lads, this doesn't look right?" as for the next mile we passed along a single carriage road through a quiet residential area. Eventually however a sign pointed to Rt1. Relief.

We ploughed on past Morro Bay and on to San Simeon. This is a beautiful stretch of coastline, a wide plain sweeping down from the hills to a benign Pacific Ocean. Reaching the jetty at San Simeon I motioned to the boys to look right. There, like a tacky wedding cake decoration, was Hearst Castle. But the low cloud afforded only the briefest of glimpses and the boys seemed uninterested.

And it was then on to the Pacific Coast Highway proper. Perhaps the light was better. Perhaps it was because I was heading north rather than south. Either way the journey seemed more beautiful than the last time I had driven along it. The temperature too was much more comfortable than it had been in Solvang. But as we headed north so the mist became thicker and by the time we reached Big Sur, the sun had all but disappeared.

The Bixby Bridge, Rte 1, Ca.

MBrennand.

It was 5.00pm. What to do? Either follow John's suggestion and visit Point Lobos State Park or do the 17 mile drive. I chose the former, the fog dictating that little would be seen on the drive. And I wasn't convinced that a succession of golf courses would enliven the boy's day.

Entering the Park I was a little perturbed at the $10.00 entrance fee given that there were only two further hours of daylight. Yet my disquiet soon evaporated as I discovered that we had the place to ourselves. To Whalers Cove where we parked and took the trail around Cannery Point, to Bluefish Cove. Despite the low cloud the raised promontory looked out across the broad expanse of the bay to Pebble Beach in the distance. With characteristic understatement the blurb in the leaflet described this stretch of shoreline as "the greatest meeting of land and water in the world". I could think of some equally spectacular meeting places, the North West coast of Scotland being just one, but who am I to doubt America's self belief. For it is indeed a fact that this coast provides one of California's richest underwater habitats. And it was also clear that in the two hours available, we would barely scratch the surface of the visual feast on offer. In fact one could probably spend the whole day here and not be sated.

For all the apparent calm every now and again the quiet would be interrupted by the crash of what appeared to be benign waves but were anything but. Sea lions and otters were said to inhabit the bay, the prevalence of kelp being a particular attraction. For whatever reason most of the wildlife appeared to be elsewhere, reminding me of a bird reserve in Scotland which, whenever I seemed to visit, produced not a sighting. For all that we did catch a brief glimpse of a Harbour Seal and there was also plenty of birdlife. At Hidden Beach we joined the Bird Island Trail, aptly named due to the pungent smell of guano.

By 7.00pm it was starting to go cold and the boys were getting hungry. Back to the car where Jack entered the details of our Motel into the Sat Nav. Fifteen minutes later I was signing in at the Monterey Quality Inn. Just as well we had booked. The place was full.

Our room was small for three but clean and functional which is all that was required. On the drive in I had spotted an Italian restaurant within walking distance. Knowing that the boys would not balk at the offer of Italian food, once changed, we headed for Carusso's Italian Pizza Parlour. It was perfect. Service was friendly and well paced and the pizza excellent. More importantly we had enough left over to box up for lunch tomorrow. A fitting way in which to round off an excellent first day.

Saturday 19th August 2008

The previous evening, whilst checking in, I had asked whether breakfast was included in the price. The proffered reply, curt though it had been, confirmed that it was and a cursory wave of the hand informed me that the dining room was next door. Keen that we should get to the Monterey Bay Aquarium early, in order to avoid the queues, we were up at 7.30am and having washed and shaved descended on the restaurant. However as I opened the door it was clear that "restaurant" was to overstate matters. To begin with it was a lot smaller than I had envisaged and there was no carpet on the floor. In the middle of the room sat a row of three Formica topped tables around which were shoehorned twelve plastic chairs. And on the surrounding shelves were various stations for cereal, pastries, beverages and toast.

Keen that the boys should get a balanced start to the day I insisted that they both had a glass of fruit juice together with some cereal and I then left them free to choose from the pastries. Heeding my advice Jack proceeded to pour himself a huge bowl of fruit loops, a cereal which looked as if it contained enough sugar in one serving to satisfy his recommended weekly intake. He followed that by selecting an iced bun and by doing so achieved the exact opposite to that which was intended. In what was to become a recurring theme of our trip, I found myself getting increasingly alarmed by his choice of foods and the potential impact on his health.

We sat down and were eagerly ploughing through our food when, in walked a large unkempt figure looking not unlike Hagrid. His threadbare clothes and stale odour suggested that here was the local hobo. Advancing towards the food he proceeded to help himself to two heaped bowls of cereal, an assortment of pastries, a cup of juice and two bananas. Then, with a dexterity that defied both his size and gait, he performed a graceful exit. We just sat there in wide eyed amazement.

It transpired that our early rise was a mistake since the Aquarium didn't open until 10.00am and not 9.00am, as I had thought. Not to worry. At such an early hour we had no trouble finding a parking spot and we filled the dead time by walking down the famous Cannery Row. Hard to believe looking at all the gentrification that this was once the centre of thriving fish canning industry. There is lots to see in Monterey but our singular aim was to visit the world famous Aquarium, described in our *Rough Guide* as containing "one of the largest, most stunning displays of underwater life in the world". Such monikers are often a recipe for disappointment as the spin exceeds the expectation. With Monterey Aquarium that is never likely to happen for in its design and the quality of the exhibits it is in every way world class.

Our early start turned out to be a blessing because there was no wait to get in, yet within the hour the place was crowded. By this time however we had gained a head start on many of the exhibits dwelling at the splash zone, the reach out and touch area and pondering the lives of the wading birds many, of whom were injured and unable to fly. However top of the list of attractions for the boys were the jellyfish, Jack commenting that he found it incredible that a living object of such beauty should also be so deadly and achieve it all without a brain. I hadn't thought about that. For my part I was mesmerized by the platinum skinned tuna, a fish whose lack of effort belies an incredible turn of speed.

Were it not for the need to get back on the road we could have stayed here all day. But after a brief visit to the souvenir shop, at 12.45pm we returned to the car for our pizza. Still remarkably good.

We needed to get back to Rte 1 but without an ultimate destination to enter into the SatNav (we were going to Muir Woods north of San Francisco) we had to rely on the signs to get us out of Monterey. All was fine until, on Delmont Avenue, signs to Rte 1 suddenly dried up. I turned into a residential area just beyond El Estero Park and immediately knew that we were wrong. So, defying that age old law that states "blokes never stop to ask for directions", I stopped and asked for directions.

The intended target was a retired local who struggled initially to grasp what I had asked. Perhaps it was my accent. Anyway at the second time he realised what I had said and launched into an elaborate set of instructions indicating that we should go right here, left there and so on. However in prefacing his response with a confidence eroding "I don't drive very much these days but I think you need to ..." I chose to totally ignore his advice. When, three minutes later, we returned to exact point where I had previously flagged him down, I had to acknowledge a fundamental error in my thinking. "You prat" I exclaimed. "Perhaps he had been right after all." So this time I followed his advice and ... lo and behold within a minute were coming across signs to Rte 1 north.

I was now in new terrain, travelling through an area of white sand dunes. Prime land one might think, for a Donald Trump development.

Once beyond the dunes the land is very quickly given over to farming and I learned that Castroville, ten miles north on Highway 1, is the Artichoke capital of America – 85% of the nation's crop is produced here. By any measure a staggering amount.

Artichoke

Delicately flavoured though they may be, with a mouth watering heart, for me the artichoke will forever be remembered with a first family holiday to France. It was the summer of 1971 (I was 11, my brother David 8) and having crossed the English Channel by ferry to Le Havre, we then had a long and arduous journey to Benodet, in South Western Brittany. Two places that made an impression were the statuesque Pont de Tancarville, over the River Seine, and the town of Dinan, because of the heat. By the time we reached the latter, nerves were somewhat frayed. Never the most patient of drivers my father had taken it upon himself to pass anything and everything in his way, resulting in overtaking manoeuvres that were butt clenching in their fearlessness. Others might describe them differently but images of narrow escapes remain etched in the memory.

Shadows were lengthening by the time we finally arrived at our hotel, hot, tired and a little tetchy. Thus, when we were assigned to rooms which were not those that had been booked my father stood firm and, using the full range of a wartime school certificate in French, took the management to task. He was fiercely principled when things were not as had been agreed and we got our rooms.

What happened next however would go down in family folklore. After a freshen up and change we assembled in the hotel's dining room for dinner. It would be some time later before we sensed that a form of retribution had been wrought when the only food offered was that on a set menu – which had a very limited choice and contained as an entrée: Artichoke.

My parents had broad culinary tastes but even they were puzzled as to what it might be. Remember that this was the pre-Delia Smith, pre-supermarket era when the most exotic item to have graced the shelves of a greengrocer was a French onion. Thus when this strange purple green vegetable was placed before us we just stared at one another in total bewilderment.

The waiter, having scuttled back to the kitchen, was not available to advise and it was only when another couple on a nearby table ordered the same thing that we gained any inkling of what to do. Thus were the leaves peeled off and dipped into butter before eating the tender base. We knew nothing of the heart so failed to eat it and when all the leaves had been peeled, felt both underwhelmed and cheated by the minuscule amount that had been edible. It would be another twenty years before I learned what to do, a little late for the hotel whose dining room we avoided for the remainder of our week.

Further on in the Pajaro Valley we entered a land covered with apple orchards and these accompanied us to the outskirts of Santa Cruz, the next point on our journey. It would have been nice to have seen the famous boardwalk but we still had a long way to go and limited time in which to do it. So we headed on north along I17 a road which takes you into the redwood covered mountain range that separates Santa Cruz from Silicon Valley. Thus began one of the most unexpected and delightful passages of our journey.

From afar the names of Palo Alto and Silicon Valley are synonymous with the hi-tech world of computers, the dot com bubble, the internet and unrivalled success through global brands like eBay, Intel, Sun Microsystems, Google, Oracle and Yahoo. That they should be located in such a beautiful part of the world with a seemingly perfect climate, is enough to make anyone from Wolverhampton extremely jealous. Which it did. For a moment I dreamed of what it would be like to be a senior techie at one of these companies having to drive home of an evening in your Ferrari, to a lovely hillside home surrounded by pine and rolling hills. Beautiful wife, wholesome kids. Nirvana. There must be a downside but at that particular point one didn't readily spring to mind. Sadly a degree in Geography was unlikely to open the necessary doors into such an exulted existence. So I returned to reality by asking Jack how far it was before we reached San Francisco.

Not that it really mattered for by now we were on I280, surrounded by redwood covered slopes and within spitting distance of the infamous San Andreas Fault. This particular stretch of road is regarded as "the most beautiful urban highway in the United States" and it was easy to see why. On we pressed, passing the sparkling waters of San Andreas Lake and Crystal Springs Reservoir and into the southern fringes of San Francisco. The further north we travelled however the more overcast it became and by the time we had rejoined Rte 1 to get through San Francisco a steel grey sky had gained the upper hand.

Our goal now was the Golden Gate Bridge. I had been here on two previous occasions and on both it had been enclosed in mist. I feared a repeat, but before this could be proved we needed to stop for petrol. My choice could have been better, the forecourt of the station that I chose not being the easiest to get onto. Locating a free pump I came up against the Pay At Pump scenario which required me to key in my card details. This would have been fine had I lived in the States but since I didn't, I was unable to go beyond the question asking me for a US zip code. It would not be the last time that this request would irritate and it demonstrated how Europe, with its almost universal use of PIN codes, is so far ahead. The lad managing the site was Vietnamese and had limited English but he was accommodating enough and between us we got around the problem.

Back to Rte 1 where, for the next ten minutes we were carried along by the volume of traffic before being faced by the huge red towers of The Golden Gate Bridge. It's hard to describe their awe inspiring grandeur made all the more imposing by the eerie mist surrounding them.

Ever a happy go lucky soul, as we reached the mid-point I couldn't help but think that it would just be my luck for there to be a major earthquake, turning the whole structure into a rippling wave. Ridiculous I know but the volume of traffic meant that progress was slow and I was relieved when we reached the other side and pulled into the Vista Point.

Why, I don't know, since by now we could barely see the bridge so covered in mist was it. However, in the short term, it was unlikely that we would come here again and I wanted to record the event for the boys, by photographing them in front of it. Despite the dreary conditions the car park was crowded but we were fortunate that a couple of cars should leave just as we arrived, thus avoiding an overdue wait.

We got out and all hell broke loose. Jack had the plastic folder with all our hotel bookings down by his feet and as he opened his door, out fell the folder. It was immediately picked up by the strong wind. "Bloody hell Jack, we need to get those back" I exclaimed and off he went in pursuit the papers gambolling their way towards the icy waters of San Francisco Bay. Thankfully a kind gent managed to save two sheets and Jack proved a real star in catching the remainder before they disappeared for ever. Disaster averted.

Somewhat chastened I stowed the papers in the glove compartment and then got out to take a photograph. My goodness it was cold and the sight of the two boys freezing in their shorts made for an odd picture. It was all rather disappointing.

In his notes John had suggested taking Conzelman Drive, in the Golden Gate National Recreational Area to another vista point affording panoramic views of both the bridge and city skyline. But with nothing to see I scrapped the idea in favour of our second option, Muir Woods.

Off we set but as we drove along the winding route of Shoreline Highway, with its flashing signs warning that the car parks at Muir Woods were full did it dawn on me that I'd lost complete track of what day it was. So immersed in the responsibilities of driving, direction finding and chivvying that it never dawned on me that today was Saturday, that Saturday came on a weekend and that weekends are generally a time when people like to go sightseeing. Had I realised this I'd have probably turned around at the Golden Gate vista point and returned to San Francisco but as it was, we were on our way now and we needed something to compensate for the disappointment of being denied our vista.

On Panoramic Highway our route was still shrouded in low cloud but as we turned left on Muir Woods Road our rapid descent brought us, incredibly, back into sunlight. The transformation was bizarre.

Eventually we were directed to the car park adjoining the visitor centre. Normally in such circumstances I seek out a distant parking spot and walk rationalising that in the time it takes to drive around finding a place to park, I could have got out and been at the destination. On this occasion however I just followed signs into the main car park, which as those that we had seen previously, indicated that it was FULL. But for the second time in the space of an hour our luck was in. Being the back end of the day there were more people leaving than arriving and yet again we were fortunate in having a parking slot literally materialise in front of us.

We had arrived. Two hours later I declared it well worth the effort. Uplifting, spiritual, relaxing are just a few of the feelings generated by a walk along the well defined trails of the woodland floor. Muir Woods is a place to relax and smell the flowers, one of the few remaining redwood forests in this part of California. Apparently all the surrounding countryside had once been similarly covered until the residents of San

Francisco chopped them down to form the posts and beams of their Victorian houses.

Our karma having been replenished we headed back into San Francisco over a Golden Gate still cloaked in mist. With the aid of the SatNav we made steady progress to Lombard Street, John having said that if we got the chance we should drive down the famous squiggly section between Hyde and Leavenworth. But as we started to make our way along the straight section leading up to it, ahead was a queue of cars at least three blocks in length all seemingly waiting their turn. Having spent much of the day in the car did I now want to sit a further thirty minutes in a traffic jam? No.

To the ████████ Hotel on Fisherman's Wharf which we drove passed at the first attempt. Driving into the forecourt I told the boys to wait for me in the car whilst I confirmed our reservation.

The lobby was distinctly grander than the one I'd been in last night. There were two check in desks and a large waiting area furnished with a number of voluptuous sofas, in a style one might find in an upmarket brothel. Wandering up to the desk on the right I produced the print off to confirm my booking. "Can I see your ID?". I really do not like this question with its presumption of guilt and, in a country so committed to the rights of the individual, it remains an oddity.

"I haven't got any" I replied, irritated. "I've got my driver's licence but it was issued so long ago that it doesn't have a photo". She was just going to have to trust me.

"Here it is" I said producing the licence "As you can see it has my name and address details". These matched the details on the booking. Really. How many people from England called Brennand were likely to be checking in today? The licence also contained my signature. "Will my signature do?" I said and then writing it out in front of her I demonstrated clearly that I was who I said I was.

Eureka! The strain on her face lifted as she uttered the words, "That'll do".

There followed a description of how to find our room, the issuing of our key and instruction on what to do with the car, which needed to be parked in the multi-storey next door. It was unclear at this stage whether the fee for parking would form part of the overall room rate.

Back at the car I found the boys absorbed in their Nintendos. "Lads, we need to unpack here, and I'm then going to have to park the car in the car park next door whilst you wait for me in the lobby. Okay". Silence. So I said it again. Still silence. "Hello! I'm not going to say this again. Get moving or I'll take those things off you and you won't get them back until we are on the road again." At last. A response

Hidden Costs

I'm not going to argue that where service is concerned Britain is the crème de la crème. Nor for that matter do its hotels offer the best value for money. But when you book a hotel room in Britain the price you are quoted generally includes a breakfast. At the ▮▮▮▮▮ Fisherman's Wharf this was not the case and nor would it be at a number of other hotels where we would subsequently stay. No doubt they would argue that there are lots of local outlets that offer breakfast. That is not the point. When staying at a hotel I have no wish to leave it in order to source the first and arguably most important meal of the day. You didn't have to do so here, it's just that if you chose to eat *breakfast at the hotel's restaurant you had to pay for it. When I was subsequently issued with a further bill for $60.00 to cover two nights parking, I was not best pleased. To quote a room rate which bears no relation to the final cost is underhand.*

San Francisco may be a cosmopolitan city but it also easy to see on foot and more importantly safe. In fact the complete antithesis of LA. Having settled into our room I returned to reception to ask for directions to the nearest Indian Restaurant. After a quick discussion I was pointed in the direction of Columbus Avenue but finding the aptly named "Indian Curry House" took longer than planned. When finally located we entered by what was clearly the rear door. With no Maitre d to greet us I was unsure of the protocol so just sat down at the nearest table. In the States such things don't really matter and it wasn't long before a waitress noticed us.

Ordering food for children often presents a problem, particularly if there is no children's menu and you are in unfamiliar surroundings. And so it proved here although why I didn't get them to share a dish fails me. Perhaps I was thrown by what they interpreted as onion salad in yoghurt sauce to accompany our poppadoms. What I got was a huge plate of tomatoes and lettuce which was not really what I was looking for. I then compounded the error by ordering three naan bread and rice which, together with our meat dishes, formed a daunting mountain of food. Before long the boys were overwhelmed, having consumed barely half what they had ordered and even my considerable appetite couldn't reduce all that was before us. For once I just had to accept defeat.

Back to the hotel for 10.00pm and a brief update from the Olympics. NBC coverage is dominated by the remarkable exploits of Michael Phelps, who yesterday became the first athlete to get eight gold medals in a single Olympics.

Sunday 20th August 2008

To breakfast. The restaurant at the ████████ is sited in a rather nondescript room on the second floor. It had but one window, which was positioned in such a way that it was difficult to see out of it from any of the dining tables. The set up was managed by what appeared to be a Vietnamese couple whose grasp of English was at best rudimentary. If this were not a barrier to comprehension then the self-serve-style menu, with its myriad options and price points, was a conduit to total confusion.

If I was merely baffled this was but nothing to the apprehension foisted on the restaurant staff who were forced to maintain an eagle eye on all diners to ensure that they only ate the food that they had ordered. Things came to a head when Jack, whose option included a banana, decided that having got it he didn't want to eat it. So I ate it, but a banana did not constitute part of my chosen option. As I ploughed innocently on a look of horror took hold on the face of management. "He doesn't qualify for a banana" she thought until the penny dropped. The whole thing needed rethinking.

And so to our day. During the early planning of our trip this was the one day that concerned me. For all its reputation as a city for challenging established norms – the beatnik generation of writers, gay rights, free love – where young children are concerned San Francisco is a sober place with nothing akin to Disneyland, Sea World or a world famous aquarium. There is of course Alcatraz but you need to book up early for the limited number of tours and I hadn't done that. So the challenge was how to keep them interested through a day of sightseeing, albeit around a city which is not only pleasing on the eye but also located in the most beautiful of settings.

From experience of dealing with my two I have found that it helps if you forewarn them about what will happen whilst at the same time giving them something to look forward to – in this instance lunch in Chinatown. They seemed happy with this, so off we went. First stop, the quirky section of Lombard Street, to experience some of what we'd missed yesterday.

The first thing you realise when moving about on foot is just how steep – and I mean really steep – are San Francisco's streets. And the second thing you realise is how much of where you walk is made up of residential property giving the city a civility not always experienced in large metropolitan areas.

As we commenced our ascent of Hyde Street the air was cool, but the large areas of blue sky hinted at a lovely day ahead. Hyde Street is particularly steep and as such provides wonderful views across the bay. In the distance I pointed out the towers of the Golden Gate Bridge – ironically visible today – and in the bay the outcrop of Alcatraz.

At the intersection with Lombard Street we reached a convenient plateau. To the left were the fabled curves, to the right a long line of cars waiting to test their brakes. It was only 10.00am yet the place was busy, tourists crawling everywhere and like me trying to acquire the ideal shot. It's actually quite difficult to get the ideal shot, so steeply does the road fall away. I could have climbed on top of one of the walls that embrace it but felt that such a course of action might be rather unseemly. So I pondered my options and whilst looking around my eye was caught by the serene sight of a local resident reading the Sunday paper in his study. The contrast with the commotion outside could not have been starker but I couldn't help but think that, whilst he might live in a lovely house on a beautiful street, it came at considerable cost.

Lombard St, San Francisco

M Brennand

We began the descent on the set of steps that run either side of the street but as we reached the half way point from behind there came the anguished cry of an irate Italian woman. Turning around the car she was driving was stuck at the top of the road, rather in the manner of a ski jumper who has lost their nerve. And then beneath her the sound of skateboards as three young lads attempted to slalom their way down. It was a suicide run and sure enough at the second bend all three of them crashed somewhat inelegantly into the delightfully manicured box hedge that lines the road. It is no doubt illegal. Which probably explained why, within an instant, they had gathered up their boards and were gone.

Next stop Coit Tower a dominant presence in the picturesque area of Telegraph Hill. It was built with money bequeathed by Lillie Coit in 1929 as a tribute to the city's firemen and at 212ft high looks alarmingly like a fire hose nozzle. Rumours of Coit's liaisons with firemen have stoked theories that it might have more to do with another part of a fireman's equipment. Not that I explained this to the boys as we negotiated the steep slope of Filbert Street, with its brightly coloured clapboard houses and scented gardens.

Walking in San Francisco is to be encouraged because at all points you can look back and admire the views. Furthermore parking around Coit Tower is limited and to my mind there is nothing worse than getting near to where you want to be only to find that you have to drive around for ages to park your car. On my previous visit I was unaware of a lift to the top of the tower because Catherine and I had failed to ascend it. This time it was a must, if only to provide another diversion for the boys. There was not too long a wait so I bought tickets and joined the queue. Somewhat surprisingly, given French antipathy towards America, we found ourselves amongst … you've guessed it; a gaggle of cheese-eating surrender monkeys. Who said the nuances of diplomacy were dead.

As luck would have it our wait for the lift was short for, being a three, we were suddenly and rather unexpectedly plucked from the line and taken to the front as a sort priority package. Like the lift operators the lift itself was old and it creaked and groaned under the weight of all those who were crammed into its small floor space. Once at the viewing platform we burst out like peas from a pod into the sunshine. Up a short flight of steps to the viewing area proper where there is a series of glass windows from which to observe the city and surrounding bay. The weather could not have been kinder and with little in the way of pollution we could see for miles.

Fifteen minutes was more than enough sightseeing for the boys and with a rhetorical "can we go now?" we headed back to the lift.

Trans America Pyramid, San Francisco

MBrennand

To Jackson Square via North Beach, and its refined Italian delis. Unfortunately, what remains of San Francisco's historic district was disappointing. Whilst the area of redbrick buildings has been sympathetically restored there was no "square" to speak of and little in the way of street life. Given more time I might have wandered around a bit more but, not unreasonably, the boys were getting tired since I'd taken them on a rather circuitous route to Chinatown. It being near lunchtime I therefore assured them that we would now look for a restaurant.

After New York, San Francisco's Chinatown is the largest Chinese community outside Asia. Its origins lie in the Chinese labourers who came to the city following the completion of the transcontinental railroad and the many sailors who came to benefit from the Gold Rush. Not that the locals offered much in the way of friendship, submitting the incomers to a series of vicious racial attacks and in 1882 passing the Chinese exclusion act which banned new immigration and resulted in thousands of single Chinese men being forbidden from either dating local women or bringing their wives from China. The law of unintended consequences quickly followed as a vibrant prostitution and gambling quarter developed, controlled by local gangs known as tongs. It took until the Second World War, when China sided with the US, for the rules to be loosened. This, together with a predisposition for hard work, has transformed Chinatown into the vibrant success that it is today.

Entering the area via Grant Avenue one is immediately struck by how lively the place is. And of course, the unique architecture. Getting here was the easy bit. Choosing a suitable restaurant was another matter since it soon became apparent that we were spoilt for choice. Having nothing in the way of a recommendation I settled on the age old adage of looking to see which establishments had the highest proportion of Chinese diners. After two false starts we finally settled on the Four Seasons, ascending the blood-red carpeted staircase to a huge first floor dining area. In no time at all we'd been shown to a table and before I'd had chance to get settled a pot of Chinese tea was placed before us.

Such is the spread of the Chinese Restaurant brand that, had we been transported from outer space, it would have been difficult to know whether we were in San Francisco or Birmingham, England. The set meal is a familiar option and with children to feed, invariably a good choice. One might say that we had sufficient.

By 2.30pm we'd finished and I suggested to the boys that we went back to our hotel for an afternoon siesta before going out again in the evening. Well I had a rest. They watched the NBC coverage of the Olympics which at every commercial break appeared to carry an advert for ED. "What's ED dad?". America is such a strange mix. The bible bashing right with its puritan sensibilities and the liberal left with its support for gay rights. And here on a terrestrial channel, where any form of nudity is still banned, were adverts for Erectile Dysfunction. And on a Sunday afternoon. Unbelievable.

By 6.00pm it was time for another wander, to work off some of our lunchtime calories and to justify a final meal of the day. To Ghirardelli Square, where most of the shops were on the cusp of calling it a day, followed by a wander up Van Ness Avenue. Then to Lombard Street again, for one final look, the line of cars still backed up two blocks awaiting their turn. It was dark by the time we left and headed back to Subway, for our evening meal. The boys' choice. So that, as they say, was San Francisco. The City where the New World begins. We'd sampled a mere slice, but I for one had enjoyed it. Perhaps this holiday was turning into what a holiday should be – a real break.

Monday 21st August 2008

On any normal Monday the regimen that typifies the start of the week is normally accompanied by the combative tones of the BBC's John Humphrys, skewering some hapless politician until they flounder in a mist of obfuscation. The *Today Programme*'s regular time checks keep us on task.

- 7.00am wake Jack.
- 7.15am, downstairs to make Jack's breakfast.
- 7.30am Tom up and together with Jack washed.
- 7.50am – Jack out the front door for his lift to the school bus.
- 7.55am – Breakfast for Tom and me.
- 8.35am – walk with Tom to see him across the main road from where he walks the remainder of his trip to school.
- 9.00am – weekly shop for groceries.

But this was not a normal Monday and getting up was not the usual military operation and having got up we made our way along the hotel's soulless corridor to sample the delights of another breakfast. Being our second visit bestowed upon us veteran status but, unfortunately, things were still as confusing as they had been the previous day. Despite my best intentions once again Jack managed to procure a health free option. And once again there were eagle eyes watching what we ate.

In his "guidance notes" John had suggested that it would be better to delay our departure from San Francisco so as to avoid the early morning rush hour. So it was in relaxed mode that we departed our room to pay the bill which finished some way north of what I'd first anticipated. I'd resigned myself to having to pay for the parking but that, plus the room tax (which I'd not allowed for) and the two breakfasts took it to $190.00 over and above the quoted room rate. Irritating but being typically English I withheld any complaint. Stupid really.

Our journey out of San Francisco took us along the Embarcadero, passed the gentrified quayside to I80 and the substantial form of the Oakland Bay Bridge. There is no toll on the outward journey which probably explains why you are confined to the tunnel like surroundings of the lower deck for the entire crossing.

Living somewhat in the shadow of its more glamorous neighbour, the Oakland Bay Bridge is no less a marvel of engineering. Work on crossing the bay to the east of San Francisco began in 1933 and by 1936, at a total cost of $77m, the work was complete. Back then the bridge also carried two lines of railway but, by 1963, these were removed to make way for an additional two lanes of traffic. There are now five in both directions. During its long life the Bridge has undergone major changes and importantly survived a couple of earthquakes, the most recent in 1989 when a 50ft section of the upper deck collapsed causing a single fatality. The 'quake, which measured 6.9 on the Richter Scale acted as a wakeup call and in January 2002 work started on replacing the Eastern Span with a new cantilever bridge. Unfortunately the project has been dogged by funding shortfalls and budgetary overspend. If all goes to plan, and it's a big if, the work will finally be completed in 2013 at final cost of $6.3 billion. Which just makes you wonder how they completed the original in just three years.

We were now at the outskirts of Oakland a city that for me will forever be associated with the Raiders, that most loved of NFL franchises. So loved in fact that for a period in the eighties and early nineties they decamped to Los Angeles. Living as I do in a town where the local football team has been turning out on the same patch of land for over 100 years, I will never understand the NFL franchise system. Supporting a local team is like a marriage. There are good times and bad, great highs and extreme lows. But through it all you stick together, creating a bond which only those who have experienced it can understand. Which makes the transfer of a team to another city, merely on the whim of an owner, the cruellest of acts. At least the Raiders, however unloved, are back where they should be. Oakland's other claim to fame is that it is the final resting place of the 546 unclaimed souls, who tragically died in the massacre at Jonestown in the South American jungle. Home for the Unloved, might be its raison d'être.

Once off the Bay Bridge we were faced with a myriad number of signs and, with no clear view of where we needed to go, we chose the wrong exit, heading in the direction of Berkley when it was Yosemite that was our destination. Performing a volte-face at the first available intersection got us back on track, I580 being our required route.

For a time we travelled through pleasant suburban districts, all of them served by the Bay Area Rapid Transit system, whose track ran parallel to our path. And as the houses and shopping malls became ever scarce, so did the BART come to a sudden halt at Dublin/Pleasanton Station. Leaving it behind so woodland became ever more scarce and rolling grassland more prominent. We were entering the northern end of the San Joaquin Valley, California's bread basket.

Regarded as the most productive unnatural environment on earth almost a quarter of all the United States' agricultural production comes from California, and the vast majority of this from the San Joaquin Valley. Yet in a strange dichotomy it is also one of the most polluted areas in the State. Hemmed in by mountains and rarely having strong winds to disperse the smog, the pollution comes mainly from diesel and petrol fuelled engines together with farming operations such as dairies and field tilling. So bad are things that it regularly vies with Los Angeles for the dubious accolade, "Most polluted area in the United States". Not sure what that says about the nutritional value of its produce.

The route to Yosemite is not as straight forward as one might think since it is some time before you begin to see signs directing one in its direction. Whilst Jack's map reading skills are good he is still young and might not always choose the most appropriate highway although had I had a little more faith in his ability I'm sure he would have been fine. That said as we drew close to Manteca I had to check the map for belt and braces reassurance. We were fine and now embarked on a long and featureless stretch of highway that took us through what I imagined were mile upon mile of walnut grove. Eventually they gave way as we commenced our climb into the foothills of the massive Sierra Nevada Mountains. By the time Groveland was reached we were well and truly mountain bound and the sight of a petrol station prompted a stop to fill up. For some time now I'd noticed an exponential rise in petrol prices as each station was passed. Groveland had the feel of the last staging post after which petrol would be scarce and even more inflated.

The tank suitably filled, it looked like an appropriate place for lunch. Unfortunately, bar a couple of restaurants in the high street, there appeared to be no store where we could buy sandwiches or pizza. I was reluctant to shell out on lunch so we deferred, not for the last time, to the bag of nibbles that Judy had given us back in Ojai and went to a shady park just off the main highway to eat them. Our timing was impeccable, a large tourist bus having just loaded up and driven off as we pulled in. Who needs a Michelin Star restaurant when an outdoor picnic table amongst woodland is on offer? With the temperature a balmy 70°f, we could have stayed there all day. But a destination beckoned and, after an hour, we were off again.

One thing you can guarantee about children is that they don't always react with a level of enthusiasm that you would anticipate. On seeing Yosemite for the first time, some thirty years ago, its combination of beauty and grandeur, hit me between the eyes. I therefore reckoned that it would have a similar effect on them. Granted they are somewhat younger than I was when I first came here and they weren't seeing its splendour from Glacier Point. However we were still faced by a series of breathtaking views and stopping to take photographs I pointed to Half Dome and El Capitan. But, to my disappointment, they appeared underwhelmed. And, following a third stop for photographs there came a world weary "Can we get back into the car now".

Eventually our route took us onto the valley floor with its rocky riverbed, grassland meadows and giant Sequoia.

Further on we reached the vast block of El Capitan bright sunlight rebounding from its white granite rock face. Set as it was against a backdrop of clear blue sky it was high definition viewing. And it is here that you start to gain a sense of the magnitude and beauty of Yosemite and understand why the photographer Ansell Adams devoted so much of his life to capturing it on film.

Something of an Alfred Wainwright is Adams. Wainwright was an eccentric Englishman who devoted thirteen years of his life to documenting walks on every single fell and mountain in the English Lake District. He loved the peace and solitude that the landscape offered but in printing his idiosyncratic guides he brought the region's beauty to a mass audience and was thus responsible for a huge boost to the tourism that he so loathed. "Man destroys the thing he loves most" and I suspect that Adams had the same effect on Yosemite.

The traffic into Yosemite Valley had been nothing more than I had anticipated but when we arrived to check in at Curry Village the place was heaving. Being unfamiliar with the surroundings I had to work out where we checked in and, having done so, how we were to get our belongings to our cabin. Not for the first time I was getting ahead of myself, living life in the future which is not a great way to be.

In spite of the long queue to check in, the Main Office was well staffed and we were not long in being served. Yet again I was asked for ID and yet again I had to explain that my driving licence didn't include a photograph and I would get my passport but it was currently hidden in the depths of my suitcase. Accepting this explanation the Ranger asked that when we were unpacked would I mind showing him my passport for verification. Okay fine. He then embarked on a list of do's and don'ts most of which was dominated by the threat from Brown Bears. The list of items to remove from the car included: food, sunscreen, deodorant, hairspray, conditioner, shampoo, air fresheners, ice chests, bottles, trash and crumbs, toothpaste, soap and last but not least canned goods. That would be everything, then. Having finished I was asked to sign a damage waiver. Apparently bears break into more than a hundred cars each year a statistic which, if intended to instill paranoia, certainly succeeded. Once I had parked the car I spent a good fifteen minutes scouring every pocket and surface to ensure that it was "clean". Even then I wasn't convinced. Was that a small crumb of pizza on the front passenger seat?

We had been allotted Cabin No 258 and like all the other hard sided cabins it was both basic and snug. At little more than 10ft wide and 14ft long it was furnished with a pair of double beds, a chest of drawers, a chair and a recess which acted as on open air wardrobe. There are around 730 of them together with 80 plus canvas tent cabins and when I went back to the Front Office to show my passport, I gained a sense of just how busy the place was. The bloke I'd registered with was having a conversation with a couple who were departing a day early and who were asking whether some people they had met that day could have their cabin for the night in what would have been a straight swap. Clearly under pressure he was reluctant to agree, explaining that, like an airline, they had overbooked the cabins and were in danger of not being able to accommodate all those who had made reservations. The couple were very persuasive and eventually he relented. I was just grateful we'd arrived in good time.

Without wishing to labour the point the big downside of visiting Yosemite at this time of year is the sheer volume of visitors. The place was full to bursting point and later that evening, as we waited in line to order our pizza, not a single table free, staff overstretched, I concluded that it could only be the most hardened walkers and climbers who would happily endure this for more than a few days. Having said that for the most part outdoor types tend to respect their surroundings and by implication their fellow man. These ideals bring with them a sense of trust, fairness and civic pride, so, whilst the queues were often long and rather tortuous, they were always ordered and the site well cared for. The volume of visitors may initially have been disconcerting but it became less so as I realised that we were amongst agreeable folk.

Before bed recorded the boys for the video diary.

Tuesday 19th August 2008

Woke to a perfect blue sky and the stunning spectre of Half Dome. Situated as we were on the valley floor, surrounded by spectacular scenery it's difficult to get your mind around Yosemite's scale and beauty and that in itself presents a problem. How best to utilise the limited time on offer. Thankfully yesterday my eyes had been drawn to an article in the Yosemite newspaper headed "Best ways to use your time in Yosemite" and listed beneath it was the hiring of bikes. Aside from the benefit of allowing us to explore much of the valley floor it also offered a standalone source of entertainment for the boys.

Thus before breakfast we went to the bike hire centre, a good decision, since the place was quiet and we had first choice of the many bikes on offer. They were strange entities, with chopper like handle bars, chunky tyres and a braking system that required you to pedal backwards to lock the rear wheel. Unusual but not that difficult to get used to. Satisfied with our choice I decided to hire them for the whole day, thereby removing any pressure to return them before they had served their purpose. As I signed the necessary forms I was on the verge of asking about bike locks when I stopped, knowing that to do so would have amounted to an insult.

Living in England, rare are the occasions when you can eat breakfast outside. Even rarer to do so, surrounded by towering granite cliffs and giant sequoia. Which is what we now did and once we'd consumed our coffee, croissant and cereal, the boys familiarised themselves with their bikes, careering around the site and practising slides on the wood chippings. I planned the day's route and packed the rucksack with left over pizza for the day's lunch.

Once ready we set off in an anti clockwise direction heading first to the Merced River from where one of the many routes up Half Dome begins. The bright sun cast eerie shadows as it passed through the canopy of woodland and every now and again we'd pass the dead hulk of a fallen redwood. I'd read that for some years now the park authority had pursued a policy of leaving any fallen timber to rot, there being a prevailing view that trees tend to support a greater degree of biodiversity dead, than alive. In such a state not only do they provide vital soil nutrients but they are also used by mammals as pathways, bridges and places to shelter from potential predators. However, in summer, this mass of rotting wood becomes tinder dry and now so much of it that it poses a significant fire hazard. This would be fine were it not for the vast number of folk who visit the valley and it is not for nothing that the park authority was in a heightened state of alert during our visit.

As the valley of the Merced River came into view, from a distance it looked a grand affair. It was just that over its bed ran a rather timid trickle of water. It was the same at Mirror Lake which is only a lake in winter and early summer. The puddle before us was rather sad. To get here we had to leave our bikes and set out on foot, following a path which runs alongside Tenaya Creek. The news that they were going to have to walk prompted pained expressions from the boys. But, as is often the way when they demonstrate initial resistance, once we got to our intended destination, they thoroughly enjoyed it; and inevitably by the time I was ready to depart it was all I could do to prize them away from the selection of huge granite boulders whose slippery crust they spent climbing up and sliding down.

Returning to the bike park it was gratifying to see that all twenty or so bikes that had been left unattended were still there. I'm not sure such a circumstance would prevail long in Britain. The world views us through rose tinted specs; a nation of genteel manners, croquet on the lawn and cucumber sandwiches. The reality is slightly different, for not for nothing did we build an Empire and deliver to the world football hooliganism.

Off we continued on our loop now heading in the direction of Yosemite Village. Before long we crossed the Merced River again, now moving through a languid section, banked by shale and sand. Seeing an opportunity to throw stones we stopped and the boys wandered off for ten minutes to practise their skimmers.

I watched from the bridge only to be joined almost immediately by what looked like a group made up of two families, all riding bikes. "This is where we swam last year" announced the mum before continuing "It looks fine … c'mon we are here now…". As she tried to cajole her troops I sensed a distinct lack of enthusiasm. "Are you sure this is where we came?" said another followed by "It's still not very warm …." a claim that was hard to dispute, a thin band of cloud now blocking out the sun. "It's not too cold" said the mum but with limited conviction. The obfuscators were gaining the upper hand and then, without even dismounting to test the water, they were off, swim deferred for the time being at least.

Whilst this little scene played itself out I was conscious of a couple on the bridge deck, binoculars trained at the huge rock face in front of us. They were clearly looking for rock climbers and having brought my own set of glasses I joined them. "Can you show me where they are?" I enquired. The woman pointed to a small tree which, incredibly, had made a life for itself on the sheer granite face. "Do you see that tree?" she said before continuing "find that and then if you pan up to the right at about two o'clock you should be able to see them." I did so but because I didn't really know what I was looking for it took me a while to locate what appeared to be the outline of a woman, tucked into a vertical fissure. The woman I talked to said that there were four climbers in all. By following the rope from the first figure I could locate her colleagues, three in all, two above and one below. It was a shock to see just how small they appeared, almost Lilliputian, against this vast edifice and watching their deliberate progress, resting one minute, moving with great care the next was fascinating. I suffer terribly from vertigo and only marvel at their exploits. Before long we were surrounded by a gaggle of folk eager to get a look. Even the

Half Dome, Yosemite

MBrennana.

boys seemed interested, throwing stones having now lost its allure. But, however hard they tried, they couldn't direct the glasses to the correct spot. Basic binocular control a skill still to be mastered.

After ten minutes we moved on, leaving our fellow observers to entice others to stop and look.

Reaching Yosemite Village there were visitors everywhere so we headed on to a spot just beyond Yosemite Creek where the bus stops for those who want to wander up to the foot of Yosemite Falls. Here we found a quiet area for lunch and sat down to eat the remains of last night's pizza together with Judy's nibbles, still going strong. Within minutes we were surrounded by chipmunks. Well I think they were chipmunks, one of which came and sat on my thigh and looked longingly at the thick slice of pizza that I was enjoying. Initially enchanting these little animals soon became highly irritating our cause not helped by feeding them peanuts which only served to increase their brazen persistence. The novelty soon wore thin and it was only when we'd finished the pizza and I put the peanuts away that they let us be.

The *Rough Guide* describes the Lower Yosemite Falls as "magnificent (in May and June)". This being August I still walked the short distance to its base from where the only indication of its existence is a dark stain on the rock face. Even in its dormant state it was easy to imagine its power at the height of the snow melt runoff.

By the time I returned to the boys they were happily engaged sliding off yet another rock on which there was a naturally formed chute. I gave them the five minute warning before we set off again this time through the accommodation at Yosemite Lodge at the Falls. At time the bike trail was a little vague but eventually we got back on the right track and as we did so the wooden lodges gave way to the most glorious grassland meadow. For a brief moment there was not a soul in sight and I used the opportunity to take a number of photographs, a singular pine providing a focal point of interest.

Unaware that I had stopped the boys had continued on, and it was some while before we met up again on the footbridge over the Merced River. Here its slow meandering passage had formed a wide sand bar which was serving as a beach. In the bright sunshine it was a popular spot for sunbathers, paddlers, swimmers or those just looking for a place to relax and let the world pass by.

"Why don't we go back to the cabin get changed and return here later?" I asked to which the response was positive. We therefore headed back to our cabin passing on the way the oddly named Housekeeping Camp. This lay adjacent to another stretch of beach on the Merced and being closer to our cabin I suggested that it might be better if we came back here when we were changed.

That said I wasn't entirely sure whether we could do so, since Housekeeping Camp gave the impression that it was reserved for the staff who worked in the valley and was therefore off limits. That fear was soon allayed as we entered the camp with its booking office, restrooms and shower blocks all bearing a close resemblance to those at Curry Village. Finding the beach, its secluded location explained why it was far less crowded than the one we had spotted earlier. The boys prepared to brave the icy water and I settled down to read *Tears of the Giraffe* the second in Alexander

McCall Smith's enchanting ladies detective agency series. I had to admire the two of them for at their age I would have been nowhere near the water. For the most part the river was barely deep enough to swim but eventually they did take the plunge to cries of anguish as their bodies were encased in the cold water.

Just down from where they were swimming the river flowed over a naturally formed causeway a fact that was apparent to only the few. And even those who did so still chose their route with great care, fully dressed as they were, bar footwear. It was whilst I was watching the tentative progress of a group of three that I spotted a brown bear moving through the trees on the far river bank. It seemed incredible that he should show himself not only in daylight but so close to the valley's main car park. Unfortunately just as I whispered to the boys "Look there's a brown bear" a group to the left started shouting and screaming at the top of their voices. Clearly startled, with a couple of bounds he was gone. Thanks for nothing.

We stayed at the beach until 4.00pm when it was time to return our bikes. They had more than fulfilled their role.

Yesterday, as we had queued for food, I struggled to reconcile the valley's beauty with the number of tourists. Now it's safe to say that I can.

Wednesday 20th August 2008

It is perplexing how little I remember from the trip Catherine and I did on our honeymoon in 1988. Back then we had entered Yosemite from the east, via the Tioga Pass but little if anything of its grandeur do I remember. More troubling, given its size and desert location, is my total lack of recall of Mono Lake. In mitigation this may have more to do with the direction of travel which from the south denies the driver a raised aspect. Thus today, we experienced the most diverse and striking day of our journey so far.

It began early under another cloudless sky and following a light snack for breakfast we vacated our cabin early and went to check out. I cut a strange sight as I pulled our huge wheeled suitcase through the camp site, but fortunately I was not alone. There was no charge for the spare key that we had lost on the beach at Housekeeping and having settled the bill we returned to the car. Relieved that it hadn't been damaged I threw the suitcase into the boot and we were off.

The Tioga Pass (Rte 120) or Tioga Road as it is more commonly referred to by those living locally, splits Yosemite National Park in two. It was originally a wagon road built in 1883 by the Great Sierra Consolidated Silver Company and had remained relatively unchanged until 1961 when realignment and improvement brought some of Yosemite's most stunning country within the reach of the car driver. We joined it just west of Valley View and for a while travelled in the opposite direction to that which is required. Eventually as the road winds its way from the valley floor an eastward direction is reached. Thankfully the traffic was light allowing me to make frequent stops for photographs, one being of a remarkable glade where at least half the trees had been literally snapped in two. They looked like broken cocktail sticks but what had been the cause of the devastation was not entirely clear, since I wasn't aware that tornados occurred here.

As we pressed on huge slabs of grey and white granite became ever more prevalent until we eventually reached Olmstead Point what might best be described as the back door to the Yosemite Valley.

Olmstead Point.

MBrennand.

It is a mind boggling spot almost as if a glacier had literally passed through that very morning leaving behind vast swathes of exposed granite rock. The view point offers one of the most spectacular vistas anywhere in the park and it was hardly surprising that there should be so many people here. I couldn't help but notice a bus load of Spaniards who, tired from their journey, were sunbathing on the wall edging the lay by. Yet more photographs before we were mobile again.

Whilst my outward expressions of grief have receded with time, every now and again something happens to trip me up. And it's usually a number of factors that combine to bring it about. As we passed along the shoreline of Tenaya Lake the scenery, the lack of Catherine to share it with and the melancholic tone of a Pat Metheny track somewhat aptly titled "Tell her you saw me" all combined to cause a huge wave of sadness. My eyes filled with tears as I found myself thinking back to the late eighties when every year we would drive down to the South of France singing along to the music of Pat Metheny. How she would have loved to have been with us now.

The stretch of road that we were driving along was one that Ansell Adams had attempted, albeit unsuccessfully, to prevent from being upgraded. At that particular moment, I was pleased he had failed because the driving was easy and there were marvellous views. I toyed with stopping but, as each lay-by was reached it was invariably occupied, so we drove on. Actually I'm not a great stopper even when I know it to be a sensible course of action. I like to get to where I'm going but in so doing can often miss real gems. This almost becoming another case in point.

Beyond Tenaya we reached Pothole Dome on the eastern fringe of Tuolumne Meadows. At 8600ft this meadow in the sky is a beautiful space, river, grassland, trees and granite peaks merging with sublime grandeur. If truth be known we had arrived at the wrong time of year, July regarded as the peak of visual perfection when the wildflowers finally emerge from their winter slumber in a blaze of colour. It still looked lovely to me but being in non stopping mode I was almost at the point of passing right through when my eye was drawn to the odd sight of the a dead conifer tree resting horizontally on its branches. Beyond it was the shimmer of the Tuolumne River and beyond that a trail leading to the large white form of Lembert Dome.

Stopping the car in a makeshift lay-by I climbed out, crossed the road and followed a track up to the conifer. The light was so clear and the air so clean that it was just too good to pass and I decided that we should now have lunch. Before long the three of us were settled amongst an area of scrub shaded from the intensity of the sun by a small coppice of trees and listening to the trickle of water behind us. Upstream, two fly fishermen were hard at work, their lines a constant blur as they flicked them up and down from the water's placid surface. It was beautiful.

Once again the pizza provided an excellent lunch and having finished we wandered down the river, the bed of which was for the most part exposed due to the lack of water. We had fun throwing skimmers and pottering around clambering over a set of stones that formed a natural crossing point. After a while I returned to the car with a "We've still got a long way to travel today and it's getting on so you've got another ten minutes before we need to be moving again". I got something in the way of an acknowledgement but wasn't convinced that they had truly listened. When ten minutes later they still hadn't returned I started to get agitated. Children have an innate indifference to time and as if to prove the point, there they were happily pottering about, not a care in the world. But, just as I was at the point of setting off to fetch them, they hurled their last stone and started to make their way towards me.

We now began our departure from Yosemite and as we headed further east so the land became drier, the vegetation more sparse and the landscape more bleak. The Tioga Pass Road descends gradually and as it does so in front of you appears Mono Lake. Travelling towards it you cannot fail to miss it and just short of the intersection with the 395 there is a vista point which, had we had more time, I would have taken in. I regret this now, as I do not driving down to the lake shoreline to see the Tufa Towers. It was only later, in the comfort of our motel room, that I learned of their status as top of the 32 things not to miss when visiting California. Oh well, can't do everything.

Mono Lake is fascinating and not just for the combination of size and desert location. For much of the second half of the twentieth century it has been at the heart of a David and Goliath struggle over water rights.

In 1941 the Los Angeles Department of Water and Power secretly extended an aqueduct system into Mono Basin. The effect was to divert water from draining into the lake and as a consequence evaporation of water from the Lake surface exceeded inflow. Oblivious to the environmental damage that they were causing in 1970 the City of Los Angeles built a second aqueduct and the water dropped even faster. By 1982 Mono Lake had lost almost a third of its 1941 surface area and the once submerged Tufa towers on Negit Island had become connected to the mainland by a causeway. The island is the main breeding ground of the rare Californian gull and in being connected their nests fell prey to a range of predators. They fled the site.

In 1978 David Gaines, a student from Stanford University who was researching the Lake, formed the Mono Lake Committee. They in turn joined forces with the Audubon Society to protect the Lake through public trust laws. Their efforts finally prevented the City of Los Angeles from diverting water with a positive effect on the surface level. However, it still remains some way below the 1941 level. You would think such a beautiful and unique feature would be protected in perpetuity. Not so. In 2014 the rights to the water come up for renegotiation.

A few miles on from Mono Lake we passed through a small coniferous wood, where fire had recently raged. Few if any of the trees had been spared. And these sad exhibits were almost the last gathering of trees that we would see for the next two days, the desert terrain of the Mojave now being our constant companion. The boys seemed enthralled since we were now experiencing scenery that is unknown in Western Europe. The vast scale and the lack of human habitation are hard to grasp, yet even here amidst this desolate environment it was not long before we came across human life. I120, our route, was undergoing repairs and as we hit the start of the section of work we were greeted by the generously proportioned figure of a labourer holding a stop sign. A convoy system was in operation but, this being America, it was not over 200 yards as might be the case in Britain but more like a couple of miles. All of which we could see down the road ahead. We had just missed out on the last run and had something of a wait before the convoy returned so I wound down the window. "How yer doin'" said our man through a mouth concealed behind a mass of facial of hair reminiscent of one of those characters from ZZ Top. "We're fine" I replied "How are you?" and then as if stating the obvious "Hot work I would guess?" He just nodded. There was a pause, into which I inserted a follow up "How long have you been working out here?" "Just about a week now. We're behind schedule. We should've started work on the 395 but with one thing and another". I noticed what looked like half a caravan strapped to the back of his pick up. "Are you living in that?" I asked pointing to the truck. "Yep". "What even out here at night?". "Yep". All we could see was mile upon mile of brown arid desert, split by this fissure of tarmac road. Not my scene but I bet the night sky was good.

Our somewhat stilted conversation over, within minutes he was being drawn into action as the convoy returned. Spinning his lollipop with a deftness that belied both his age and girth his board now read "Go". We were off.

Our next human interaction came at Benton Hot Springs, pop. 13.5. Believe me that's what it said on the sign. Did it mean that at the last Census one of the populace was a baby and thus didn't yet qualify for full status. Or more alarmingly did it mean…. At least Benton Hot Springs had a general store where we could stock up on water so I sent the boys to find out, reasoning that it would be a good experience for them. When, five minutes later, there was no sign of them I started to get worried. Had they been kidnapped by some sinister cult whose motives didn't bear thinking about? It was then that I caught a glimpse of them in the store preparing to pay and the next minute they were bounding towards me laden with liquid.

Off again and before long we reached Rte 6 and headed north in the direction of Basalt. And within fifty miles or so I was announcing, to whoops of excitement, that we were crossing the Stateline into Nevada. We were on the same ground yet new ground.

It was 4.30pm by the time we reached Tonopah. Initial impressions of the town, built on the mining of silver, were favourable since the first building on its outskirts was a smart new Burger King doubling up as a petrol station. I needed fuel and having behaved so well the boys deserved a treat in the form of an ice-cream. It was such a relief to drive into the shade offered by the canopy covering the petrol pumps but, as on previous attempts, the pump would not work until I had prepaid. I couldn't do that at the pump because I didn't have a Zip Code. So I wandered into the store where I was greeted by the smiling face of middle aged woman. I explained my conundrum and then with a degree of initiative that belied her short tenure (she was in her first week of employment) she asked to keep my card and told me to go and fill up. Which is what I did, returning when I had finished to pay for the fuel and to add three choc ices to our order. By now I had moved the car back into sunlight. The heat was oppressive and to consume our ices in the car would have led to a rapid thawing with the potential of cream everywhere. So we moved to the shade at the side of the building where even here it was so hot that our ices were soon losing their form. Not that it prevented me taking in the scenery if one could call it that. Next door to the filling station was another building, again relatively new but unlike the station no longer in a state of financial health. It looked like it had once been a motel but the rooms were empty and from inside came the intermittent sound of hammers dismantling furniture. Or that's what I assumed it to be.

Either way, perhaps Tonopah was not quite as prosperous as I had first thought, a view that became more credible the closer we got to the town centre – if four derelict buildings at a crossroads could qualify as such. It had all the feel of a town on the verge of extinction, for never have I been to a place where there were so many failed businesses. And yet, with no shortage of land, rather than re-occupy these buildings or knock them down to build new ones, the clear policy was just to carry on building out leaving a desolate hole at the centre. It was a Polo in urban form.

Our home for the night was another Best Western Motel which, once again, I missed on our first run. Quite an achievement given that it is one of the few large buildings not in a state of disrepair. Behind it was a large spoil heap and derrick which formed part of an extinct mine. Yet more evidence of decline.

Parking the car we made our way to the reception desk to sign in. Pleasantries and booking confirmed what I wanted to say to the receptionist was; "How come Tonopah is such a dump", but I couldn't quite carry it off so what I actually said was "Are times tough in town at the moment?" "No" came a tired reply, "this is pretty much how things are. We go up and down with the mine and things are not that great at the moment." Had she continued I sensed it would have contained a dose of implacable American optimism. What she did say however was that the military had a base close by where they test the F-117 Nighthawk. So not totally dependent on the mine.

Tonopah may have been clinging to the last vestiges of life but for all its shortcomings what it did have was a Laundromat. With four days still to go I had run out of socks and shorts for the boys and underwear for me. It was a most welcome sight particularly since it was within walking distance of our motel. All that needed to be washed could be gathered up into two large supermarket carrier bags and with instructions to the boys to bring their books, off we went.

Best Western, Tonopah NV.

M.Brennand.

Not that initial impressions were promising. Aping the general air of decline, of the ten washing machines that were available only two worked and of the eight tumble dryers only three were in working order. Fortunately we were not alone for an aged couple from Kentucky (I know this because the licence plate on their car said so) were in the process of finishing off a wash and transferring their clothes to a tumble dryer. I enquired what I needed to do to get the machines to work and they kindly took me through the whole process including how much I would need and pointing me in the direction of the petrol station next door where I could get change and washing powder.

Before long our clothes were revelling in the soap and water of the front loading tub and I was sitting with the boys making friends with George and Nancy. I break the ice by telling them that back in 1981 I nearly went to University in Lexington and that gets them talking about Kentucky and where they come from; the mining area in the SE of the State. They are doing what many of their generation now do – get in the car and drive. Today they had arrived from Utah en route to Tucson, Arizona. One might describe them as part of the undemonstrative backbone of America, whose parents, universally regarded as the "the greatest generation", went to fight the Nazi tyranny during World War II. They believed in God, disliked gays, thought the country needed a morality check, wanted the troops out of Iraq, felt disenfranchised by politics and didn't much care for either McCain or Obama; and, most importantly, they admired our Queen and knew of her regular visits to Kentucky for The Derby.

As our conversation unfolds they probably wonder why a chap with two young lads is on his own in a Laundromat and when I tell them that my wife had died two years ago of breast cancer they look shocked. Experience tells me that the mere mention of this fact tends to hasten an end to conversation almost as if those to whom I am talking consider it impolite to continue. And so it is here although the discourse is drawing to a natural conclusion. Removing their last item of clothing from the tumble dryer, Nancy announces. "That's it" and as she sets off to leave she places a strip of fabric conditioner in my hand a gesture which I sense says more than the comment which accompanies it. "It will make your clothes smell nice".

The laundry done it was time to eat so we head to Tonopah Station and a meeting with our friends from LA. (ref opening chapter). In both its decor and food it was like a throwback to the cultural desert that was the seventies. But it had a charm all its own and the service was excellent perhaps spurred on by the knowledge that they'd got three visitors from England. Returning to our motel room that evening I could think only good of our Tonopah experience.

Thursday 21st August 2008

In *The Lost Continent*, Bill Bryson's classic travelogue through small town America, he opens his tale with the quote "I come from Des Moines, Iowa. Somebody has to" which of course is delightful but slightly unfair when you compare Des Moines to the settlements in this south western corner of Nevada.

Having pricked our conscience I'm reluctant to run Tonopah down. But that still leaves the small matter of "quality of life". Limited though my perspective might be, to live here with any sense of mental wellbeing would require a character of tempered steel. And, if Tonopah engendered such thoughts, they were as nothing compared to the quaintly named Goldfield, whose urban squalor we would pass through some thirty minutes later. Hard to believe that during the first decade of the twentieth century it was a thriving gold town and, for a brief period, the largest town in Nevada. But, like a grape shrivelling on the vine, when the gold dried up so did the town. And what remains is very much the rump of that rush.

At the last census in 2000 there were 440 souls who still lived here yet all I could think was "How?" The dilapidation, the lack of water, the heat, the dust and the barren and monotonous landscape. Viewing it through my suburban-centric gaze it had little if anything to commend it. But who am I? The residents of Goldfield might think it beautiful.

This was a day of stark contrast; Tonopah being the start, Las Vegas the finish. In between we embarked on a tour of Death Valley for me a journey of redemption.

Here's why. Allow me briefly to turn the clock back to

Thursday 2nd October 1986. Waking that morning under canvas at Mesquite Springs Camp Ground, I was looking forward to a hot day in Death Valley. But, as I poked my head through the tent flap, above was a steel grey sky, a feel of rain in the air. And before I'd dismantled my tent, it had indeed started to rain. And it continued to rain, albeit lightly, all day. That's right … all day. A rare and unique occurrence, but a disappointing one, since it was to experience heat that I had come. I felt cheated. But as we headed south along I95, with not a cloud in the sky, salvation appeared close at hand.

Reaching Scotty's Junction we turned right and began our descent into the Valley proper. Our first destination was Scotty's Castle and in the thirty minutes it took us to get there not a car did we pass. It's a strange unnerving experience for though I had prepared well by filling up with fuel and stocking up on water, I kept thinking about Gus Van Sant's disturbing movie, *Gerry*, in which two lads get lost in Death Valley, with tragic consequences. If we break down might a similar fate befall us?

As our descent towards the valley continued so did our altitude, quite markedly in parts, the road passing through a series of narrow canyons. Just short of Scotty's Castle we were confronted by the bizarre sight of a tract of green scrubland made up of reeds and bushes. Beneath ran a stream which forged a route down to the entrance for Scotty's Castle. Here the sight of a pristine lawn added to the surreal air. The castle is in fact a mansion built during the 1920's by Albert Johnson, a wealthy Chicago insurance broker, as a desert retreat. It remains unchanged from the day Johnson died in 1948 and I read somewhere that its luxurious interior is a popular attraction. During the winter months hordes of tourists queue to view its' delicately carved wooden ceilings, and crafted tiled floors. But being summer, the place was deserted.

Tom, Uberhebe Crater, Death Valley.

MBrennand.

To Uberhebe Crater a corner of the valley which, with its particles of dark ash and oxidised minerals, looks for all the world, like a lunar landscape. One might think that a hole such as this can only have been created by a meteor but it is actually the remains of a volcano dating back a mere 2000 years. Getting out of the car we were hit by a blast of hot wind. It was literally akin to standing in front of a huge hairdryer and at last I was experiencing the heat that makes Death Valley one of the hottest places on earth.

The reasons are two-fold. First altitude or rather lack of, which at Badwater descends to 282ft below sea level, (the lowest point in the western hemisphere). Second, its position in the rain shadow of four surrounding mountain ranges reducing annual rainfall to a mere inch and a half.

The low altitude coupled with a lack of shade, combine in raising temperatures to unbearable levels.

Yet its name is a misnomer. Whilst the environment is unforgiving humans have lived in the surrounding area for over 10,000 years. Back then the valley was a Lake, the climate being mild and supporting a wide range of wildlife. By 1849 it was as it is today and in that year the first non-natives attempted to pass through the valley en route to the Gold Rush towns west of the Sierra Nevada. Despite running out of food and water they managed to survive but it was the death of one of their number that gave the valley its name. In the ensuing years it was only miners who were prepared to brave the hardships of living in such an inhospitable place. Whilst gold, silver and copper were all found it was borate, a harsh alkaline used in detergents and soaps, that proved the most successful mining endeavour. So much so that by the late nineteenth century twenty mule-team wagons were employed transporting borate ore across the desert to the railroad line at Mojave.

Although at the point of leaving Uberhebe Crater we'd been in Death Valley for over an hour we had still to pass through an official entrance point. This was soon reached as we headed along Rte 267 to Furnace Creek but there was no-one in attendance. I got out where a sign read "Entrance fee $20.00". I am hard wired to be honest and duly paid believing that at some point evidence that I had entered the valley on valid grounds would be requested. I was wrong, but at least my conscience was clear and I trust they put the money to good use.

267 is the main route along the length of the valley but despite its prominence there was little in the way of traffic. I

stopped frequently to take in the brutal beauty of the place where the surrounding hills are worn away in fantastical shapes and colours. At face value one might think it impossible for life to prosper, but it does, snakes, fish, eagles and bighorn sheep managing to eke out an existence. And dotted everywhere the Creosote Bush on whose straggly branches sprout tiny resinous leaves which are built to withstand both heat and drought.

It was by now nearing mid day and incredibly hot. On the regular occasions that I stopped I made sure to leave the car running, partly to keep the air conditioning going but also to remove the risk that the engine might not bring itself back to life. Being from more temperate climes, the boys found it too hot and it was only when we reached the Centre at Furnace Creek that they wanted to get out.

Although small by American standards the visitor's centre is fascinating, full of interesting artefacts and displays including an excellent topographic map of the valley and its surrounding hills. It is well worth a visit and not just because the air conditioning system is brilliant. I could tell that Death Valley had made a big impression on the boys and before we left they bought a couple of t-shirts as souvenirs.

Outside we stopped by a plaque on the wall indicating that we were 190 feet below sea level. To the side was a thermometer which read 44°C in the shade. That was more like it.

We now had a decision to make. Did we want to head on to Badwater or exit the park and make for Las Vegas. The boys found the conditions too hot and thus chose the latter. On Rte I90 I made one final stop at Zabriskie Point. Yet another of Death Valley's forbidding and otherworldly landscapes. These are badlands, bone dry finely sculpted, golden brown rock, where only the sparsest vegetation can survive.

And that was it. Our day in Death Valley but one which had provided a proper perspective. Next stop Las Vegas. There now began a monotonous drive punctuated by the interest offered up by Creech Air Force base and shortly after the forbidding facade of a correctional facility. That these should even register as points of interest says something about the bleak terrain. Which continued until we transcended a rise on Highway 95 and there, rising from nowhere, were the gleaming towers of Las Vegas.

Vegas is the complete antithesis of Tonopah. Superficial, tacky and vain yet vibrant and thriving. It is like nowhere on earth – a city where none should exist.

Summoning Jack into action I got him to assemble the SatNav and insert the address of the Monte Carlo. For some reason I'd formed a mental picture of a quaint hotel on the edge of the main gambling district. But as the SatNav directed us onto the famous Las Vegas Strip and indicated that we were 800 yards from our hotel, it dawned on me that my assumption was way off kilter. When we finally arrived I was shocked to be faced by a huge monolith, almost Eastern Bloc in design, that marked it out as one of the huge casinos that straddle The Strip.

As we drew up to the front door a vast army of bellboys, almost all Mexican, were eager to move luggage and park cars. I have no idea what constitutes a reasonable tip and fearing embarrassment ignored all offers of help, choosing to unload our luggage and park the car myself. Only with completion of the latter could I finally relax, the task of driving into a big and unfamiliar city having been successfully accomplished.

Back to the hotel lobby where the boys are sitting quietly next to the luggage playing with their Nintendos. There are times when they are a godsend. We go to check in and are greeted with a service desk that has more in common with the check in desk at a major international airport than a hotel. Not all the booths are occupied so I joined a queue. Having pre-paid over the internet it was a relief to be spared the usual request for ID. Paperwork complete, we were directed up to the 23rd floor. The contrasts with Tonopah are everywhere.

For all my earlier contempt for the Monte Carlo's Eastern Bloc sensibilities, the room was both spacious and comfortably furnished clearly reflecting the amount of money that is generated by gambling. It has after all, a mere 3,002 guest rooms and 259 suites.

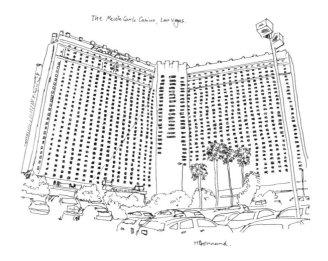

The Monte Carlo Casino, Las Vegas.

M Brennand.

From our lofty perch we had an excellent view over the New York-New York Hotel and Casino with its collection of replica skyscrapers and roller coaster, whose regular cargo of patrons provided the boys with a source of entertainment.

After a number of days in which our evening meals had been modest affairs, it was time for a treat. A challenge to which Vegas, with its metropolitan feel, was likely to be equal. So after a shower we got dressed up and headed for the bright lights. Now 7.00pm it is still oppressively hot and as we reach The Strip it is unrecognisable from the place I visited back in 1983. Block after block of huge casinos and still more going up. Scant evidence yet, of the credit crunch. I was partial to French cuisine so headed for the charms of Paris, ahead of those of New York and Venice. Is it any wonder that only 10% of Americans possess a passport. The sidewalks are heaving with tourists and street hawkers many of them selling call girls. The boys don't like it. The heat, the crowds, the traffic, the hawkers and the tawdry tackiness. They would rather be in Tonopah.

At Paris Casino I book a table at the Mon Ami Gabi. To dine al fresco is a forty minute wait. So we opt for inside which gets us straight in. Our waiter for the evening is the smarmy Bob. We order and as each choice is made he replies; "That's a very good choice, my friend". It's the "My friend" that grates and when he does it a third time Tom leans over and whispers "That bloke's too nice." I cannot disagree.

The fawning aside, our food is good, particularly my steak which I wash down with a glass of claret. There is no rush and we take our time. But before long I'm getting cold, the air conditioning being too effective.

It is time to go – bill settled and out into the heat again

for a short walk passed the Flamingo where two girls – fully clothed I might add – fake a pole dance above one of the crap tables a sight that prompts the boys to avert their eyes in embarrassment. We then cross to Caesars Palace and finally to Bellagio. The casino's are all so similar; rooms, gambling, swimming pools, spas and entertainment. It is hard to know what distinguishes one from another and perhaps explains the outlandish facades. With two young boys in tow you soon realise that this is not really a place for children. But it is also unique and has to be experienced.

At least Bellagio has its fountain, which we watch through a couple of shows. Sentimental and captivating in equal measure. Perhaps the one place, in this veneration to mammon, that provides some spirituality.

Back to the Monte Carlo and a wander through the casino, which is packed. We head for our lift and are joined by a chap whose movement is characterised by those twin ailments of old age; a list and a limp. He is overweight, but who am I to cast doubt on his build as he kindly holds the lift door open for us with a rhetorical "you got it?". We clamber on board. His friendly smile offers benevolence but it jars somewhat with the slogan on his t-shirt "I spent all my money on beer and women – the rest of it I wasted".

Time for bed I think.

Friday 22nd August 2008

After a gentle rise, to the Starbuck's concession for breakfast. Croissants and orange smoothies which are verging on the healthy. Today we were heading for the Grand Canyon, on what I knew would be a slog. An intensive study of the map ensured that we escaped Las Vegas error free, heading in the direction of Boulder City which we soon reach. It is not a big city and it takes but a short time to drive through it. And having done so one is faced by the surreal sight of Lake Mead. Descending rapidly to the Hoover Dam the whole area is currently a building site, the construction of an awe inspiring flyover being well underway. When complete it will mark a major feat of engineering carrying US 93 clean over the valley of the Colorado River and thus by-passing the bottleneck caused by the dam.

The boys didn't want to stop, claiming it was too hot. But since it was the only scheduled sight of interest between here and the Grand Canyon, I forced them to join me for a walk down to the dam wall. It's an imposing sight which at its completion in 1936 was the world's largest electricity-generating station and largest single concrete structure. It still casts a huge shadow over the Colorado but the experience, sadly, is wasted on the boys. After the briefest of looks they want to get back to the car. We wander back up the rampart like stairway which affords excellent views of the lake. Following several years of below average rainfall it is well below its expected level threatening water shortages in Arizona, California and Nevada. Not good then for Mono Lake.

We then drive… and drive… and drive until Kingman is reached at around 1.00pm. Here we stop at a Taco Bell for lunch. It is such good value that we all have seconds. And then it's on again, heading East on I40 which starts to climb and as it does, so the landscape gets greener and increasingly occupied by woodland. By the time we stop for fuel at Williams we are at 6,000 feet and surrounded by pine trees. The temperature here is gorgeous which possibly explains why Williams is a popular resting place for trips to the Canyon. We are nearly there.

The final sixty mile stretch to Grand Canyon Village is long and straight with amusing signage "Keep lights on during the day – and also at night". And within the hour we are pulling into the Village, but it's not really a Village for there are no residents here, the highway straddled by national hotel chains and restaurants. Locating our hotel, a Best Western, we sign in and are soon relaxing in our room perhaps the best that we have stayed in. John's reservations have been faultless.

Sunrise and sunset are the times to view the Canyon. I didn't reckon on making the former so after a brief break, in which the boys watched the television, I told them that we were off to the Canyon to watch the sun set. They played their face but this was not the time for negotiation. They were going – period.

To Mather Point and a view which they struggle to comprehend. The sheer scale of the canyon, the silence and that contrast. We are surrounded by many folk, all of them incredibly quiet, no doubt humbled by what they are seeing. The clarity of the light, the vivid colours and the shadows. It is in every way one of the world's wonders.

Grand Canyon

r.Brennand.

Anticipating that once the sun had disappeared there would be a mass exodus we left promptly to avoid the rush. It was a good decision because back in Grand Canyon Village we were able to both place our order and find a table at the We Cook Pizza and Pasta Restaurant. Half an hour later the place was overrun with those who had clung on to watch the sun's final death throes.

Later, at the hotel I enquired about the availability of helicopter rides over the Canyon tomorrow. Prior to coming away a good friend had said that if we got to the Grand Canyon "you must take a helicopter ride. Brenda thought it was wonderful".

For as long as I can recall I have had an aversion to helicopters. I know of too many folk who have died in them. Yet I know this fear to be unfounded, since the ratio of deaths to flights is likely to be very small. However as the preferred mode of transport for the rich and famous, when accidents do happen, you tend to hear about them; Vic Morrow, Colin McRae and Matthew Harding for example. So now we were here and Brenda (67) had said how wonderful it was, how could I return home without saying we'd taken a flight?

I'll sleep on it.

Saturday 23rd August 2008

Dear Catherine

I took a leaf out of your book today by taking a risk and spending more than I otherwise ought. In the morning, following breakfast, I booked the three of us onto a 30 minute helicopter flight over the Grand Canyon. As you know I am a cautious soul so the decision to spend a lot of money doing something which worried me was a form of double jeopardy.

We spent the morning touring the south rim, for the boys a bridge too far; another visitor's centre, another photo opportunity, another view. They seemed intent on irritating one another, which was a shame given the magnitude of the surroundings.

A lunchtime picnic amongst the trees quelled the discord before we returned to our hotel and then on to the airport for our flight with Papillon Airways. Checking in and watching the safety video only served to heighten my sense of apprehension and made me question what I was doing. Before long we were being divided into groups that would ensure equal weight distribution on the helicopter. Thus Jack went up front, whilst I went aft with Tom and fellow tourists from France and Germany. So far from home yet surrounded by historic enemies.

Within minutes of settling into our seats we were taking off and as we climbed into the air so my fears abated. Now and again a slight judder would cause the odd flutter, but for the most part it was a smooth and stress free experience. I loved it, as did Jack but Tom was less sure, looking apprehensive throughout.

We were issued with headphones partly to drown out the click clacking of the rotor blades, but mostly for the commentary. English came last but with limited quality. It didn't matter. The stunning views told their own story.

We were in the air for 30 minutes, more than enough time to appreciate the wonders of this incredible hole. And when we finally landed it is hard to say which was the bigger joy. The flight itself or overcoming a long held fear. Emotionally high, I made easy prey for those selling souvenir photos. Rare to have us together on one photograph.

Back to the hotel for a short spell, swimming in the pint sized pool before an evening meal at Wendy's. The budget's exploded – we need to cut costs, not that the boys complained. They'd be happy to eat there every night.

What a day.

All my love

M

Xx

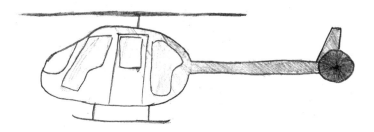

Tom's drawing of our helicopter

Sunday 23rd August 2008

Facts	Arizona	UK
Size (sq miles)	113,909	93,000
Population	5,130, 632	60,975,000
Highest Point	Humphrey's Peak	Ben Nevis
	12,643ft	4,406ft
Min age for unrestricted		
Driving licence	16	17
Min age for gambling	21	18

I had an inkling that this would be a long day so I made sure we were up early in order to be on the road by 9.00am. Even at such a relatively early hour the breakfast buffet was crowded and slightly chaotic. But it came with the room and having earlier complained about the inequities of not including breakfast in the room rate it would be churlish to do so now. The 9.00am target was achieved and we retraced our route of two days ago by heading for Williams where we joined I40 for a few miles before taking 89 to Prescott.

This was an unexpected delight, the raised altitude producing an abundance of pine. And unlike the British politician with which it shares its name, it was surprisingly attractive. It had the feel of a town on the cusp of expansion.

Fuel being low I stopped for petrol, this time being spared any niggles with my credit card transaction. I was conscious that we would be seeing John and Judy again today and wanted to buy them a gift by way of thank you. Slipping into American vernacular I asked the woman who ran the petrol station "Can you tell me where I can find a Liquor Store?"

"Yes there's one not far from here. It's called The Liquor Barn and ...." off she went with a series of directions which were clearly enunciated but totally confusing. "Thank you" I said before returning to the car attempting to keep all that she had said in some semblance of order. Off we went and at the point where I thought I she said "go right" I went right only to discover that I was wrong. I returned to the main highway drove a little further along it and went right again. Again wrong and after a tour of a couple of adjoining blocks I decided that my quest was fruitless I resigned to buy the wine at another store somewhere else. However once back on 89 we soon reached the thriving town centre where instead of bearing left on 89 I went straight on. We were again wrong. However, in attempting to get back to where we should be going there, as if by magic, appeared the aforementioned Liquor Barn. I couldn't help but smile.

Laden with wine the road out of Prescott began to descend rapidly to a verdant plain that stretched out as far as the eye could see. We were well and truly way out West. And as we did so, once again the scale of this huge country hit home.

Close to the town of Congress we missed our turn and ended up in the German sounding Wickenberg. It was midday and we needed food but there was no sign of a Taco Bell or some other cheap eatery. So I drove on in the hope that we might find something in Aguila. Again, nothing. So on to tiny Wenden, population 1000. Not a good pointer that our search might end here. Until on the left there appeared the enticingly named, Crystal's Cafe. I pulled in and as the boys opened the doors our air conditioned cocoon was overpowered by an incoming rush of heat.

I wasn't quite sure what to expect as we entered the Cafe. Bar two members of staff it was empty. Which one is Crystal I wondered? They were seated at a table in front of the main servery, reading what I assumed to be a local paper. We take our seats in one of the booths. Interior aesthetics rank low as a priority, a large industrial air conditioning unit occupying a recess at the far end of the room and tables surrounded by gaudy plastic seating. The place has a rather tired, down at heel look.

The young girl (let's call her Donna) welcomes us. She can be no more than twenty but is confident and before we utter a word, my two are being plied with a couple of huge Sodas. We are hungry and have come to the right place, with a menu containing plenty of substantive food. For once I suppress my desire for healthy eating ordering burgers for the boys and a BLT for me. By now Donna has recognised that we are not from these parts and out of nowhere she asks, "What grade are your boys in?".

I have to think. Believing that we have adopted the US system of year groups I say " Jack is just about to start Y8 and Tom Y6." She is listening but her next statement, perhaps indicating the presence of a grasshopper mind, bears no relation to what I've just said. "I would love to visit England" she says.

I then say "If I told you that England is smaller than Arizona yet has a population of 47 million people, you will get some idea of just how small we are and how many people are crammed into our tiny island." Not surprisingly she struggles to get her mind around this concept as, yet again, my chat up technique falls at the first hurdle. I never could flirt.

A call from behind the server that our food is ready spares any further embarrassment. When Donna returns it's a relief to see that the portions are just the right size. So often in the States the servings are too big, instilling a sense of defeat before you've even begun. My BLT is perfect, as are the French fries (chips) which are crinkle cut – I've not seen chips like these since my mum used to make them back in the 70's. Which is possibly the time warp in which Crystal's Cafe is stuck.

When we are finished Donna returns to clear away. Somewhat whimsically she says "I'd also love to visit Rome one day; and Ireland." Not countries you would readily pair. "Italy is beautiful" I offer. "It's my favourite European country and one you should definitely visit. Ireland is also lovely if a bit wet." I pay the bill and with thoughts on writing up our trip I need a photograph of the three of us standing next to the Dodge. Maybe Donna can help, so I ask.

She seems unsure, perhaps wondering about my motives, but eventually agrees. Outside the heat is stifling. "Do you make a living from the Cafe?" I ask believing her to have a share in the business. Her answer confirms not. "Just about. I get $3.50 an hour for waitressing, which I do three days a week. However one day a week I work at the grocery store next door and that pays $7.00 an hour". "Only $3.50 an hour?" I ask, astounded. "Yes it's the minimum wage but I can top it up with maybe $10 – $20 dollars a day in tips. It will require a lot of saving to be able to afford to go to Italy" she says with a smile. Yes I think before she follows it up with the killer. "I've got a three year old son. My boyfriend helps out

… but" and her voice then drifts away perhaps recognising that the dream of going to Italy might be just that – a dream. I feel genuine sorrow.

Uneducated, underpaid and living in the midst of nowhere, what opportunities did life offer? The land of dreams America may be but there are many thousands of Donna's, trapped in the grim realities of their existence.

"Thanks for taking the photo" I say "and I hope that one day you get to go to Rome." We get back into our now scorching car and as we do so I can't help but offer the boys the benefit of my advice "That girl lads, is a classic example of someone whose life choices are limited by a lack of education." I'm not sure they were listening.

For some time prior to Wenden the prevalence of succulent cacti and the heat had indicated that we were back in the Mojave Desert. From now until Palm Springs the journey was hard going, the type of driving that I had imagined dominating the holiday. All I wanted now was to get to La Quinta where John and Judy have their second home. They had very kindly offered to drive out from Ojai to meet us. For a time a huge thunderstorm provided a diversion, trying to assess whether it would hit us or not. Reaching the outskirts of Palm Springs I asked Jack to assemble the SatNav and enter the necessary details. And lo and behold it led us exactly to where were we wanted to go. To someone still using an A-Z I find this incredible.

John and Judy's La Quinta home is no less delightful than the one in Ojai. Modern in its square design it backs on to one of the many golf courses. Surprisingly despite our desert location the air was thick with humidity, the result of too many swimming pools – 40,000 at the last count – which have altered the climate. At this time of year the prevailing breeze also carries with it the unpleasant smell of sulphur which emanates from Mexican manufacturing plants to the south. It was becoming evident that summer is not really the time to visit. Fortunately the house had air conditioning and knowing of my English love of tea, no sooner had I settled in than Judy was presenting me with a cuppa.

Palm Springs, Swimming Pool.

MBremmand.

What a bonus to be able to stay with friends on the final leg of our journey rather than another hotel room. The boys were soon in the pool as was I before our attention was attracted by a Black Widow spider whose nest had been disturbed our splashing around. Thankfully it moved to higher ground, rather than taking to the water itself, which would have been interesting. In the evening we were treated to a tasty plate of pasta during which we provided a detailed account of our journey. And the more we talk the more we realise just how brilliantly it had all gone.

Monday 25th August 2008

Slept until 9.00am when I got up for breakfast – bacon, eggs, blueberry muffins, mango, tea and coffee. No hidden charges here.

The boys wanted to swim. I wanted to see Palm Springs. John wanted to work. Ideal. He can keep an eye on the two of them while Judy and I go for our tour. We take Rte 74 which crosses the Santa Rosa and San Jacinto Mountains, in the general direction of San Diego. It is muggy the sky thick with cloud and by the time we reach the main vista point at midday a thunderstorm is threatening. Below, in all its glory, is Palm Springs a patchwork of blue swimming pools, white villas and green golf courses. There are a few other people here, a posh biker and an English couple who, from their accents, are from London. The chap looks troubled, circling his shiny new Dodge, like a stressed blackbird whose nest has been plundered. He is locked out of the car. Everything they possess, including wallets, money, mobile phones, ID and ignition key is in the car.

"Can we help?" I say.

"This is mad" he says. "I got out the car to have a quick look at the view and when I shut the door the central locking tripped and we are now locked out". "Have you got a cell?" asks Judy. "No. It's in the car". "I think we are going to have to call the hire company to get them to send an engineer. Who are you with?" "Alamo" "Have you got a number?". "Sorry…. it's in the car. I can't believe this. I got out of the car and the next thing I know we're locked out". He repeats his tale again, but it's not particularly helpful.

The biker comes over. "You guys need help?" a question which only provides our Englishman with another opening to repeat his story. "Let me try the hire company. Alamo you said" but he has no signal. "I've got my cell in the car" says Judy. "Let me try". We get the number from directory enquiries but at the first attempt Judy gets lost in that void of the call centre, before the line goes dead. I then try but with the same result.

Despite our elevation it is very hot. They have no water and no way of summoning help. The car is secure so leaving it wasn't really a risk. "The best thing we can do Judy is to take them to an Alamo office in Palm Springs. At least there they will be safe, they can get a drink and with luck talk to someone who can sort things out".

"We'll give you a lift" says Judy "There's an Alamo office at the airport."

Their relief at this offer is palpable.

So, not quite the day I had envisaged. And sadly I saw little of the architecture for which the area is famous, our route to the airport dominated by shopping malls and three lane highways. That said every now and again Judy would point out some of the more famous houses, Bob Hope's with its famous palm trees being just one.

It took all of forty minutes to get to the airport where, to much relief, there was an Alamo office. Our English couple exit. "Thank you so much for your help" they say "You've been so kind". And they were gone, heading for the terminal. One of those rare interactions. An offer of help to people we barely knew and would never see again.

Back to La Quinta for lunch. The boys are still in the pool, oblivious to the effects of the sun. We've been gone three hours. They are looking a little red. Oh dear.

By 2.30pm it is time to head back to Costa Mesa. Once again John and Judy have been so generous, not only in putting us up but in making the effort to drive out here especially to greet us. We say our final goodbyes, with the offer that they must come and stay next year when they visit England.

Once more we place our destiny and my stress level, in the hands of John's SatNav. Without it the task of navigating a route through the LA metropolis could have been difficult. Not that the journey was entirely hitch free. In Riverside I nearly miss the Rte 91 turnoff, the result of not following instructions religiously. And then once on Rte 91 I overcompensate and end up in the Fast Track lane which, without a pass, is illegal. I've had a driving licence for over thirty years and have never been fined. I'm in America three weeks and I get a ticket.

But on this particular occasion it is an error which I welcome. There is a crash, which we avoid, saving half an hour.

It is a gorgeous evening as we pull up at John's house in Costa Mesa. He and Bryan come out to greet us as if we've been away for weeks. It seems like we have.

Tuesday 26th August 2008

Over dinner last night John suggested extending my car hire for an extra day, so that we could visit San Diego Sea World. Which is what we did today although, having been on the road for so long, I would have preferred a lie in to the 6.00am rise that he recommended.

The boys were remarkably good. Never at their best in the early morning they got up without a moan, perhaps spurred on by the prospect of the day ahead.

The benefit of our early start soon becomes apparent on I5 which, although busy, is jam free. And just as the gates are opening at Sea World, we arrive.

Located on the coast at Mission Bay Sea World is San Diego's most popular attraction and part of a money making empire that includes sites in Florida and Texas. Popular it may be but I find the entrance fee of over $200.00 slightly eye watering. It had to be done but whether one could say that

Shamu, Sea World

MBrennand

it is $140 worth of better value than Monterey Aquarium, is debatable.

The early rise has the added benefit of allowing us to tour the park before the mob arrives. Acutely aware of his own identity Tom's replica shirt – in the colours of Arsenal – prompts a reaction from the attendant at the Tide Pool who expresses a love for Tottenham Hotspur, Arsenal's arch rivals. He'd spent time lecturing at a college in London.

We see all the shows, the Sea Lions & Otter being our favourite and then fall for the Manatee's. The grace with which these large unattractive creatures move, is endearing.

By mid afternoon it was time to call it a day. John had suggested that on the way home we drive to Escondido to see Niki de San Phalle's bizarre sculptures. Part of me doesn't want to let him down. Another part just wants to get home. The tipping point of sightseeing fatigue has been reached.

We went home.

Thursday 28th August 2008

Today we said goodbye to our Dodge. One tends not to get too sentimental about such things but it had served us proud. Large enough to provide plenty of room. Small enough not to guzzle too much fuel.

Given the logistical problems that we'd experienced collecting the car from John Wayne Airport I was reluctant to repeat the exercise. I had however noticed another Thrifty outlet on MacArthur Blvd, which offered a more convenient option.

So, following breakfast I set off with Jack, saying to John that we would call him when we knew where we were and were ready to be collected. All very straight forward. Or so you might think.

It took 10 minutes to reach the office but as I made to turn into the compound it looked full of cars. With nowhere to park on the road I was forced to pull in, clattering over a road level security device as I did so.

Finding a space in the disabled slot, we go to the office.

It's the traditional cheery greeting. "Hello sir and how are you today?". We dance through the usual pleasantries before I ask "I ..err …collected my car from your office at the airport about two weeks ago but I'm wondering if it's okay to leave it here?".

"Sure. No problem. I just need to check that it's all in order. You've filled it up with gas?". "Yes" I nod "the tanks full." "Okay just give me a couple of minutes."

And sure enough a couple of minutes later, he's back. "Everything's fine Mr Brennand. I'll just close your account and that will be it". He keys some details into a computer after which there's the whirring of a printer producing our receipt. Handing it to me he says "Here you go Mr Brennand and you have a nice day".

And that was it. Excellent.

"Right Jack, you can now 'phone John to tell him where we are and that we are ready to be collected". This he does, but in the ensuing conversation I'm left with a feeling that Jack's explanation of our whereabouts is somewhat opaque. However I'm not too concerned and we go outside to wait.

Within ten minutes in the distance I spot John's Jaguar. We prepare to wave him down but as he gets nearer he's sticking to the middle lane and maintaining his speed. We start waving but his gaze remains fixed on the road ahead and as he pulls level he's still in the middle lane and still travelling at 30mph. "Oh hell Jack" I cry "he's going to the airport" and with that we set off in pursuit. Ahead some 200 yards is an intersection with a set of traffic lights and as luck would have it, they have turned to red. "Come on J" I shout "get moving and we might just catch him." Waiving our arms frantically and running as fast as we can, we make a comical sight but eventually draw level with the Jag. The light is still on red as we dash out into the middle lane and bang on the window. John looks up, alarmed at the prospect that he's about to be mugged. But if these are muggers they look surprisingly familiar. "It's us John" we shout stating the obvious. Relief now on his face he unlocks the door and just as the light turns to green we clamber in. I daren't think how much time would have been wasted had we missed him.

Crystal Cove again in the afternoon and later still another lovely meal.

Thursday 28th August 2008

"Only in America". The phrase returned to me this afternoon as we were driving through the elegant streets on Balboa Island. There on the sidewalk was the Californian dream; he lean, tanned and moneyed; she blonde, leggy and well endowed. That they were both well into middle age confirmed an obsession with staying young. They might therefore be somewhat disappointed to learn that it was their dog, and not they, that caught my attention. Dog is to stretch things a little. This creature was an accessory not a dog for there it lay in a purpose built pram, enjoying the midday sun. Forgive the piety but there are young children in Africa dying from a lack of clean water and here was a poodle with its own pram. Somewhere in the headlong rush for material gain I fear Adam Smith's virtues of temperance, decency and moderation, have been lost.

And before I have time to stop shaking my head in disbelief there, in the narrow street ahead, is a Hummer, blocking our way. But this was no ordinary edition. "That Hummer's been pimped up" said Tom summing up perfectly the vision before us. Perched on a huge set of tyres which displayed its underside, it was the most ridiculous sight in these narrow genteel streets. Can there be a symbol more redolent of conspicuous consumption? And as if to re-enforce that symbolism, there at the wheel was a Diminutive Wife.

The Diminutive Wife;

Common in the more affluent areas of Orange County. Identified by their decorative appearance the species is usually petite and glamorous, with blonde hair, swept back in a pony tail. A navy blue baseball cap is the preferred headgear. They are usually seen driving what we in England call Chelsea Tractors i.e.: Range Rover Vogue's, BMW X5's, Porsche Cayenne's, Audi Q7's and of course Hummer's. Behaviour is generally vacuous their main role being as glorified taxi drivers, the daily routine revolving around transporting little Kirsten and Scott to and from school. In down time they go to the gym, play tennis or have a Botox makeover. And, when a younger model takes their place, they descend on any one of a number of Newport Beach denizens hoping to trap another wealthy mate.

Long before our afternoon encounter with the Hummer I had spent a relaxing morning scanning the real estate adverts in the LA Times. Given the exchange rate I calculated that I could buy a four bedroomed house in Anaheim for £90,000. I could then rent it out to Disney visitors. Brilliant plan. Then again who would I get to look after it? Who would manage the bookings? Could I afford the rates? I'm not that wealthy. Perhaps I'll give it a miss.

Following brunch we headed down to Newport Beach for a walk. The local authority was nearly bankrupted recently by a lawsuit in which an individual dived off the pier into the sea only to break his neck. He had sued because there were no signs on the pier telling him that it was unsafe to do so. Mmm.

We spent a couple of enjoyable hours on Balboa beach where we played beach tennis and the boys got buffeted by the crashing waves. Too much for them.

Back to Costa Mesa via the liquor store where I bought a selection of wines for John and Bryan. In no way did it match their generosity, but was a necessary gesture. Evening meal out, at hole in the wall, followed by watching a DVD of the hilarious film *The Party* starring Peter Sellars as a hapless Indian actor. Burdy num num.

Waited an age to hear Barak Obama accepting the Democratic nomination to run for President but, like those television programmes that tempt you by saying "later we've an exclusive interview with…" and then leave it until the last moment to show it, I get fed up with the wait. So at 11.20pm I go to bed, leaving John to hear him speak. There is, however, a genuine sense that this man can restore the moral compass that has gone so astray under George Bush.

Brian

Friday 29th August 2008

Our last full day. I tell Tom that we are going home tomorrow. He is not pleased and there follows two hours of truculence. A sign of things to come, perhaps.

To Costco with John to buy lamb cutlets for the evening barbecue. To get there we head along Harbor Blvd, an eight lane highway which links Costa Mesa to Anaheim. It is wider than most British motorways and demonstrates just how ridiculous is the notion that we can end our dependency on the car and, by implication, oil.

As we pull up to a red light on the sidewalk to the right is a pedestrian trying to cross. You would think that being at a set of traffic lights there might be a point when all the traffic stops to allow her to cross. But with cars turning right on red and four sets of filter lights this never happens. Eventually the lights complete their cycle and once again we go to green. Our pedestrian is stuck on the sidewalk. For all I know she might still be there.

Being Labor Day weekend Costco is crowded, folk shopping for barbecue food. Not surprisingly all the lamb has sold out. Alternative required.

Crystal Cove again in the afternoon but the cloud comes in on the back of a stiff breeze and by 4.00pm it is too cool to sit out.

Home to find Bryan slaving over barbecued spare ribs. It reminds me of the Tony Roma Restaurant chain, where Jacqui and John had taken me back in 1986. Sadly it no longer exists – insufficiently sophisticated for Newport Beach palates, perhaps.

The meal finished I'm alone with John and a mellowing glass of wine. Some years ago he too lost his wife to breast cancer. How can it be? The lives of two beautiful women cut short. We ponder the likelihood of finding someone else. It's a daunting prospect, particularly for me, with two boys. They've already had their say. "You can have a new girlfriend when we've left home". But that's eight years away!

Friends proffer "advice". "You're creating too many barriers, you need to be more open" or "If I were in your shoes I'd get into internet dating". Arrggh.

Like a stubborn teenager I want to do the complete opposite and think "Just leave me alone. I don't need you to tell me what to do. I did pretty well the first time around. If it doesn't happen, so be it. That's life".

Saturday 30th August 2008

Our last day. Early morning tea, accompanied by the LA Times. John McCain's choice of running mate dominates the news. The unknown Sarah Palin, Governor of Alaska. All are surprised, including Palin.

A final brunch of petit pains, brioche and croissants. The perfect send off. A period of dead time follows waiting for the taxi to arrive. When, at 1.30pm, it finally does we say our final goodbyes. What to say? I'm English and reserved. I don't do gushing and there is nothing to add to that which has already been said. A big hug covers all the bases – cripes three weeks Stateside and I've gone native.

To LAX in 40 minutes and this time, a tip for the driver. "Have a beer on me" I say.

The baggage handlers strike is thankfully over and there are few holdups going through security.

Our flight however is delayed. Technical problems with a piece of equipment for a disabled passenger. When we eventually board the plane is packed yet eerily silent, again. I find sitting upright for 10 straight hours tiring. Advancing years, perhaps.

Land Heathrow, 7.30am. Outside there is a grey blanket of cloud. It is cool and the presence of water droplets on the cabin window indicate that it's raining.

I smile. "Welcome home".

PS

Dear Catherine

You would have loved this holiday in the same way that you were enthralled by our honeymoon in 1988. I dug out my diary of that year to see what I had written and on the 30th October it was you who had written the entry.

Sunday 30th October 1988

Memories of our honeymoon

- *LA = "Grotsville"!*

- *Disneyland = Peter Pan & Pirates of the Caribbean*

- *Hot Sunshine, cool shopping centres (deserted)*

- *LA Rush-hour (from Riverside) – at 5.00am nose to tail*

- *Driving through the desert*

- *Bristlecone Pines, White Mountains – total silence*

- *LA Dodgers Win World Series – Orel Hersheiser MVP inspired by Poohs T-Shirt (while in Mammoth Lakes)*

- *Yosemite, Tioga Pass – breathtaking*

- *Yosemite = Packed out $149.00 a bed*

- *Golden Grassland of California*

- *Mid America Oakdale + Mexican urgh!*

- *Seven Lane Freeway into SF: Poohs at the wheel*

- *Kurt's amazing warehouse*

- *49 mile drive –fog v.cool*

- *Chinese meal – spectacular Hunan and Micro Brewery*

- *Gays in Drag! Good Morning Vietnam!!!*

- *Nob Hill & Coit Tower & Lombard Street = Achy legs*

- *Fisherman's Wharf and China Town*

- *Parking debacle in Carmel – Poohs at the wheel*

- *Bat Rays and Leopard Sharks at Monterey*

- *Plush hotel in Carmel after Californian cuisine*

- *Touring Carmel Art Galleries*

- *Horrifying Hearst Castle = Jumble sale*

- *A visit to Denmark = Solvang*

- *Beverley Hills & fender bender (accident)*

- *Back to J & J = exchange car for deluxe model. Watch Mystic Pizza*

- *Cook for J & J = two sittings*

- *San Diego = Shamu and co – brilliant*

- *La Jolla house spotting.*

- *Soaking up the last rays, packing and Thai food*

- *Flying home into the sunrise*

And twenty years on here are my thoughts:

- *John's front garden = A slice of Tuscany*

- *Orange County & unrestrained development = depressing*

- *Crystal Cove + Pacific waves*

- *Bryan's cuisine and al fresco eating*

- *Ojai luxury*

- *Beautiful Rte 1*

- *Ethereal Point Lobos and guano*
- *Monterey Aquarium = Jelly fish & tuna*
- *Silicon Valley = nirvana*
- *Golden Gate Bridge = cold & fog*
- *Muir Woods = spiritual*
- *Lombard Street skateboarders*
- *Coit Tower = French tourists*
- *Hotel irritations = ID requests and room rate add ons*
- *Oakland 'burbs*
- *Groveland = lunch*
- *Yosemite = physical grandeur and tourist civility*
- *Spectacular Olmstead Point and serene Tuolumne*
- *Mono Lake – sleeping giant*
- *Tonopah – rugged charm*
- *Death Valley 44°C heat (redemption at last)*
- *Las Vegas – tacky, overcrowded and the fawning waiter*
- *Grand Canyon sunset*
- *Helicopter ride = nerve-wracking but spectacular*
- *Crystal's Cafe, Wendon = great food, vain hope*
- *La Quinta architecture*
- *Palm Springs humidity and pong*
- *Rte 74 – Good Samaritans*
- *John & Judy = generous hosts (twice)*
- *Rte 91 = Fast track indiscretion & fine*